W9-AZG-741

OREGON WINE
The Taste of

JĀNIS MIGLAVS

GRAPHIC ARTS™ BOOKS

❦ OPENING PAGE: Clearing storm over Brandborg Winery vineyards in the Umpqua region of southern Oregon. TITLE PAGE: Fall colors over Chehalem Winery's Coral Creek Vineyard near Newberg in Oregon's Willamette Valley. RIGHT: Fresh spring snow blankets Bella Vida and Knudsen vineyards in the hills above Dundee, Willamette Valley. CONTENTS PAGE: Ladybug on just-harvested Chardonnay grapes at Amity Vineyards winery near Amity in the Willamette Valley. Page 128: Looking from the shoulder of the Chehalem Mountains, the sun sets through misty fog and clouds over the fall-colored Adelsheim's Bryan Creek Vineyard near Newberg in the Willamette Valley.

Photographs © MMVIII by Jānis Miglavs except pages 12 and 13
Captions and Artist's Vision © MMVIII by Jānis Miglavs
Introduction © MMVIII by Jim Bernau
Book compilation © MMVIII by Graphic Arts™ Books

Photographs on pages 12 and 13 used by permission and credited as follows, from left to right: Jānis Miglavs, Richard Sommer, Douglas County Museum, Dick Erath, David and Jason Lett, Mike and Mark Wisnovsky, Milan Stoyanov, and David Adelsheim.

All rights reserved. No part of this book may be reproduced or transmitted in any form or by any means, electronic or mechanical, including photocopying, recording, or by any information storage and retrieval system, without written permission of the publisher.

Library of Congress Cataloging-in-Publication Data

Miglavs, Jānis.
  Oregon : the taste of wine / by Jānis Miglavs.
    p. cm.
  ISBN 978-0-88240-746-3 (hardbound)
  1. Wine and wine making—Oregon. I. Title.
  TP557.M52 2008
  641.2'209795—dc22   2008035514

GRAPHIC ARTS™ BOOKS
An imprint of Graphic Arts Center Publishing Company
P.O. Box 10306, Portland, Oregon 97296-0306
503/226-2402 • www.gacpc.com

Contents

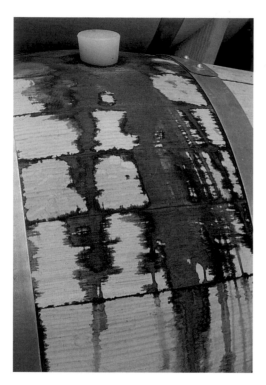

ᗧ ABOVE: Pinot noir wine stains on French oak barrels at Patricia Green Cellars near Newberg, Willamette Valley. RIGHT: Old barn and Riesling vines at Montinore Estate Vineyards near Forest Grove, Willamette Valley.

Introduction

Oregon is a special place. Her climate and soils attracted a second migration, this time of aspiring winegrowers, whose way of life has transformed the landscape.

A remarkable story is told through the lens of Jānis Miglavs and the words of our winegrowers. This book is much like the character of our industry, a collaboration of words and ideas, with Jānis piecing together well its quilted nature.

As one of Oregon's first native winemakers, it is easy to say none of what we all have today would exist if not for the contributions of the many people who made their way to Oregon to plant their vines and share their ideas. Richard Sommer, Oregon's first modern migrating winemaker, offered training by way of field seminars to aspiring winegrowers, including myself. My first introduction to wine in the early 1960s came from his bottles when my dad, a Roseburg lawyer, brought home wine from Richard, his first winery client, to share at dinner.

The founders of Bethel Heights Vineyard, Pat Dudley, Marilyn Webb, and Ted and Terry Casteel, continued building this tradition of sharing and collaboration when they spearheaded the development of the *Oregon Winegrape Grower's Guide*, the map and compass for the rest of us to follow. Inside their tractor shed, where they offered weekend viticulture seminars, I received invaluable instruction. Twenty-seven years later, it is a privilege to use the knowledge shared with me to grow Pinot noir and Pinot gris for them at Elton Vineyards.

Collaboration and respect for each other and the land is Oregon's character, shaped both by our pioneers and the newcomers noted in this book. Our early laws drafted by the Oregon Winegrowers Association, the viticultural and enological research endeavors (as embodied by Chemeketa Viticultural Center and the new Oregon Wine Institute at OSU), and joint promotional efforts such as Oregon Pinot Camp all serve as examples.

Our work to protect the land has led to progressive land-use laws, which have slowed the conversion of farmland to suburban sprawl, and to the formation of several groups to promote sustainable, environmental practices such as Low Input Viticulture and Enology (LIVE) and Salmon Safe certification. Oregon winegrowers lead the nation in the percentage of vineyard land certified sustainable, and we are working diligently to convert all remaining growers.

Camaraderie has come from these commonly held values and shared work. This is best felt in the filled chapels of one of our colleagues passing. After learning that winemaker Bryce Bagnall of Witness Tree had been diagnosed with ALS, friends and vintners organized a group called Supporters of Bryce (SOB) to raise money to help cover the considerable cost of his care. The balance remaining was donated to Chemeketa Community College to establish a scholarship in his memory. The unexpected passing of young winemaker Jimi Brooks galvanized into action winegrower friends to bring in his harvest and continue his brand and legacy for his then eight-year-old son, Pascal.

The Salud Barrel Auction, led by Oregon winemakers, supports medical care programs for vineyard workers. In this spirit, the net proceeds from the sale of this book will be donated to Salud.

My great, great grandparents, Pierre and Catherine "Kitty" Pambrun, witnessed Oregon's first migration as it was settled by early Americans. Pierre was French Canadian and Chief Factor at Fort Walla Walla for the Hudson's Bay Company, and Kitty was Cree Indian, raising nine children in the wilderness. Pierre, in his diary, recorded with anger and sadness the transformation from collaboration to confrontation and exploitation that accompanied the first migration. They would be pleased to know that the efforts of the second migration are helping to return Oregon to her proper state where we work together and walk as softly as we can on this great land.
■ JIM BERNAU, Founder, Willamette Valley Vineyards

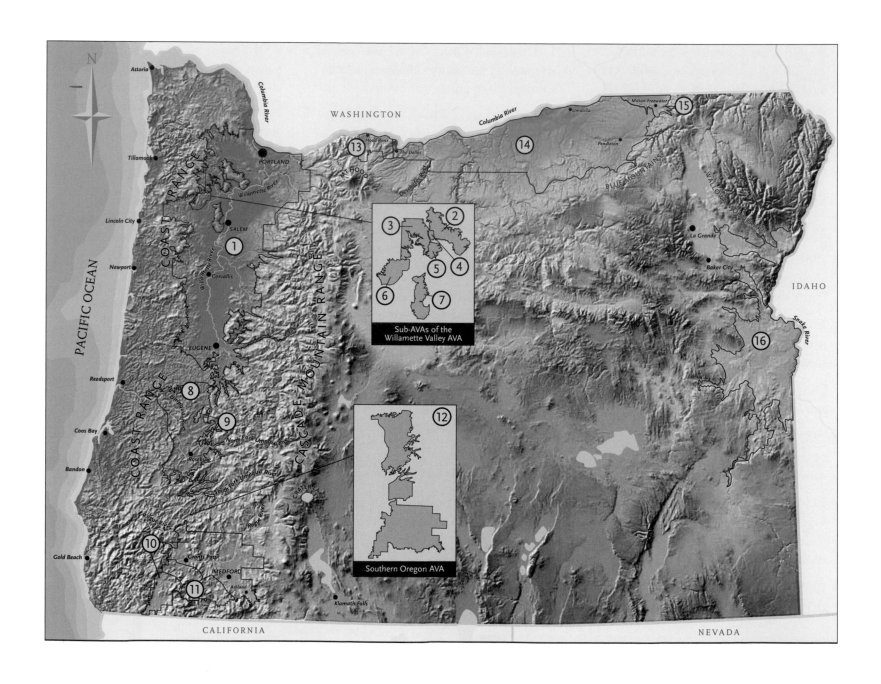

N

WASHINGTON

Astoria

Tillamook

PORTLAND

Columbia River

Lincoln City

SALEM

COAST RANGE

PACIFIC OCEAN

Newport

Willamette River

Corvallis

Reedsport

EUGENE

Coos Bay

Roseburg

Bandon

CASCADE MOUNTAIN RANGE

Gold Beach

Grants Pass

MEDFORD

Ashland

Rogue River

CRATER LAKE

Klamath Falls

CALIFORNIA

Hood River

The Dalles

MT. HOOD

Deschutes River

Columbia River

Umatilla

Pendleton

BLUE MOUNTAINS

Milton-Freewater

La Grande

Baker City

WALLOWA MOUNTAINS

IDAHO

Snake River

NEVADA

Sub-AVAs of the
Willamette Valley AVA

Southern Oregon AVA

North Fork Umpqua River

South Fork Umpqua River

Umpqua River

1 2 3 4 5 6 7 8 9 10 11 12 13 14 15 16

American Viticultural Areas of Oregon

1 — WILLAMETTE VALLEY

2 — CHEHALEM MOUNTAINS

3 — YAMHILL-CARLTON DISTRICT

4 — RIBBON RIDGE

5 — DUNDEE HILLS

6 — MCMINNVILLE

7 — EOLA-AMITY HILLS

8 — UMPQUA VALLEY

9 — RED HILLS DOUGLAS COUNTY

10 — ROGUE VALLEY

11 — APPLEGATE VALLEY

12 — SOUTHERN OREGON

13 — COLUMBIA GORGE

14 — COLUMBIA VALLEY

15 — WALLA WALLA VALLEY

16 — SNAKE RIVER VALLEY

ABOVE: Sunset reflected in Riedel Oregon Pinot Noir glass with wine.

Chapter 1

The Oregon Wine Landscape

There's no place in the world like this place right here. The soil, the weather, the hawk that's sitting down there in the Douglas fir tree that's feeding off of the gophers that are moving the soil around from this part of the vineyard to that part of the vineyard, the earth worms that are processing out the microorganisms that are breaking down last year's prunings; all of that makes this a completely unique place.

If you listen carefully enough, if you taste it carefully enough, and you come to know it well enough, you can find all of that in the wine. ■ DOUG TUNNEL

Viticulturally, Oregon is a big state. There's a lot of room to grow grapes in the Columbia Valley, Walla Walla, Columbia Gorge, southern Oregon, and the Willamette Valley, although, the north part of the valley is getting harder to find land to plant. Vineyards are spreading west in the foothills and heading south into Lane County. A lot more of the blanks are beginning to fill in, and I'm sure there'll be vineyards planted in Oregon we don't know about yet that will be just phenomenal. ■ JOHN ALBIN

ꙮ OPPOSITE: According to vineyard manager and owner, Lonnie Wright, these Zinfandel vines in Mill Creek Valley near The Dalles are growing from roots planted in the late 1800s. Every ten to twenty years the freezing Gorge temperatures kill the vines down to the roots but the vines regrow from the roots. The distant snow-covered mountains are across the Columbia River in Washington.

RIGHT: A newly planted Pinot noir vineyard with an old walnut drying barn in the background near Scholls, Willamette Valley. OPPOSITE: Snow usually falls in the Willamette Valley's vineyard-covered hills two or three times during the winter and spring. In the morning after a March snowstorm, a father and his two children crafted this snow couple next to a newly planted vineyard near Newberg in the Willamette Valley.

When I first started studying wine, had you asked me if Oregon could ever produce good wine, I would have put my nose up in the air and said, "No way. It's too cold and rainy up there. You could never make decent wines. You have to be in California to do that." So here I am. ■ JIM KAKACEK

Oregon is a geologist's paradise. It has such a rich history, with its oldest rocks formed almost 400 million years ago when this region was covered by warm seas, and our coastline was where Idaho is today. And most major geological hazards are still active here in Oregon: floods, landslides, earthquakes, erosion, and volcanic processes. ■ SCOTT BURNS, PH.D.

The Weather: that's the biggest issue in growing grapes here in the Willamette Valley, but it can be a positive and a negative. The negative is that if it rains at the wrong time you're had. The positive, of course, is having the great wines that come out of here. ■ DAVID LETT

↩ LEFT: **Shafts of sunlight break through late-summer storm clouds over southern Oregon's Valley View Winery's vineyards and production barn. Located in the Applegate Valley near historic Jacksonville, Valley View was the original name used by pioneer Peter Britt in the 1850s, but ended with Britt's death in 1906. The name was restored in 1972, by the Wisnovsky family and now run by Mark and Michael. INSET: Vérnonique Drouhin-Boss, winemaker at Domaine Drouhin Oregon, first came to the state in 1986 to intern at several wineries. When her father, Robert Drouhin, bought land in the Willamette Valley to plant a vineyard and start a winery, Véronique became the wine maker. She now commutes between Oregon and her home in France.**

Quality of life is important to us, and what you see is what you get as far as the individuals involved. The most successful people are humble, yet extremely intelligent and curious. They are always looking for ways to do things better. Oregon lacks the arrogance that you sometimes see in other wine regions. We're much more open, more spirited in that we listen to each other. There are certainly individuals with opinions, but it's interesting because over the years some of those individuals actually have started to make changes, going down paths no one ever thought they would. There is a lack of pretense in Oregon. We're here for the quality of life and because we think this is an amazing growing region. ▪ RON PENNER-ASH

↩ ABOVE: **Close up of early morning rain drops on Pinot noir grapes in the Willamette Valley. Lots of rain during harvest can be a winemaker's nightmare.**

There is the myth that Oregon is the Berkeley of the American wine industry in that we are overly intellectual and not grounded enough to make good wine. Granted, we may have started out that way, but I think we outgrew the Berkeley image long ago. The people who are making the best wine in Oregon right now are folks who are very involved in their winemaking and their growing, and pay attention to both on a day-by-day basis. ▪ TERRY CASTEEL

Sustainable practices—being good to the earth—are a core value for us. Our goal is sustainability across the operation, so we examine everything we do through the lens of what footprint are we leaving on the earth in how we farm, how we package, how we market, how we do everything. This focus on sustainability comes from the idea that humans are just part of the earth's ecology. The arrogance that we have had in trying to dominate nature is repellent to me. We are part of the process, and we need to function as part of the process. We need to not destroy other living beings in our pursuit of wealth and happiness. So we are organically certified in the vineyard. We try very hard to recycle everything we can. Even with all of our efforts, we are still very far from being fully sustainable, but we keep trying. ▪ SUSAN SOKOL BLOSSER

OPPOSITE: Fall-colored vines drop down a steep hillside to a metal barn that was originally part of the family turkey farm before the Stollers planted this vineyard on the Willamette Valley hills near Dayton. The vines are mostly Pinot noir.

We are the only gold-level LEED certified* winery in the country and the second in the world. There was one in Canada before us. There are two other LEED Certified portions of wineries. One is the barrel room at Sokol Blosser and the other is a tasting room in Napa. So those are the only ones at this point that I am aware of. ■ BILL STOLLER

The benchmark Pinot noirs of the world are from Burgundy. If you lined up three or four wines each from Burgundy and Oregon in the forty to sixty dollar price range, I think we'd kill them.

Still, there is no question that Burgundy is the capital of Pinot noir. It's where the benchmarks are set. Increasingly, however, the New World is giving them a run. It's fun being the underdog. ■ ALLEN HOLSTEIN

Many of us felt that Oregon produced much better wines than our early reputation, and were willing to challenge Burgundy to a tasting in September 1985. We selected the 1983 vintage, because Burgundy told the world it was a great vintage, and we knew we also had a good vintage that year, a very forward, rich vintage. Every Oregon winery that made Pinot noir was invited to enter into the lottery to see which ones would be tasted in New York. The International Wine Center selected seven Burgundies from Grand Cru to commune wines. They also selected ten Oregon Pinot's for this tasting.

The judges included twenty-five New York–New Jersey area experts in Burgundy, as there were few experts in Oregon Pinot noir at that time. They had seventeen wines in front of them blind, and they were asked to give the origin of every wine, plus name three favorites out of the seventeen. I believed that this would be a great marketing opportunity because our average price

*(LEED certification provides an independent, third-party verification that a building project meets the highest green building and performance measures and is environmentally responsible, profitable, and a healthy place to live and work. There are both environmental and financial benefits to earning LEED certification.)

❧ LEFT PAGE: Douglas firs at the base of their vineyard tower over the solar panel-covered Stoller winery. In addition to using solar energy, the winery became the first gold-level LEED certified winery for the use of gravity-flow winemaking techniques, energy-efficient heating and cooling, and waste-water reclamation to reduce negative environmental impact.

❧ LEFT: Winemaker Luisa Ponzi with her marketing director sister Maria Ponzi Fogelstrom uses a hydrometer to check the Chardonnay in barrels at Ponzi Vineyards winery near Beaverton, Willamette Valley. This portion of the building is the original garage from which the winery grew. The arches were the original garage doors.

at that time was about eleven dollars on the shelf and the Burgundy's was about twenty-nine dollars. I figured the Grand Cru's would beat us, and the Premier Cru's would beat us, but we would fall in the middle and would look like great value. Oregon got first, second, third, and fourth and tied for fifth. ■ STEPHEN CARY

It has been an incredibly fast learning curve in the last twenty years. We've learned very quickly from France, from everywhere else in the world. We've surpassed the masters very often because of the openness of mind and the camaraderie between the Oregon viticulturists and winemakers. Oregon is a special place in that sense of sharing. ■ LAURENT MONTALIEU

Several years ago, Earl Jones up there at Abacela Vineyards told us, "I think you guys should try growing Tempranillo in the Applegate." He's famous for his Tempranillo, and we had been thinking about trying it here. Then he says, "I tell you what, if you want to do it, call me and I'll send the cuttings down." He did. He gave us cuttings from his vineyard. You tell that story to someone

RIGHT: Early morning sun spotlights a single grape cluster and leaf in Adelsheim's Bryan Creek vineyard in the hills of Willamette Valley near Newberg.

LEFT: Wooden sign hanging at the end of a row identifying this as the 115 clone of Pinot noir in Elton Vineyard owned by Dick and Betty O'Brien in Yamhill county, Willamette Valley. OPPOSITE: Raptor Ridge Winery winegrowers and owners Scott Shull and wife Annie prepare wines from a variety of Oregon wineries for a presentation at Pinot Camp in the Willamette Valley. Pinot Camp is a yearly event where fifty wineries from throughout the state join together to bring members of the worldwide wine trade to experience Oregon wine.

in California and they're like: "He gave you cuttings so that you can make wine to compete against his?" Yep, that's what he did. And when we won two gold medals in a row, how did that make him feel? That made him feel great because now there's another great Tempranillo grower in Oregon. It's the rising tide lifts all boats theory and now maybe someone will come up to do a story about Oregon Tempranillo. ■ MIKE WISNOVSKY

While the Oregon Pinot Camp and International Pinot Noir Celebration are institutional examples of cooperation, there are lots of personal examples. One time we blew the computer board in our press right in the middle of harvest. King Estate had the same press, same size, same board. They offered to loan it to us; so in the middle of the night, we met them halfway to get the computer board. They actually ran without one of their presses during harvest so that we could continue to operate.

Here in Oregon, you'll find hundreds of stories just like that. ■ JIM BERNAU

One tragic but great story about Oregon camaraderie was the death of Bryce Bagnall, who was the winemaker for Witness Tree. He had ALS. A number of Oregon winemakers got together to form a group called SOBs, Supporters of Bryce. Everyone donated wine and did a special bottling that was sold to help the family financially. That's pretty cool. Tragic but neat at the same time.
■ JOE DOBBES

I think the emergence of the Willamette Valley as a serious world-class wine-producing region greatly overshadowed what was going on in other Oregon winegrowing regions including the Umpqua, Rogue, Illinois, and Applegate valleys, among others. Many of us in southern Oregon were kind of left in the shadows because of the amazing success of Pinot noir in the Willamette Valley.
■ MICHAEL DONOVAN

Southern Oregon doesn't get very much press. That's why we have wines called Fly Over Red and Fly Over White. Wine writers will go to Napa and Sonoma, then they fly over us to the Willamette Valley. For four years we were telling the *Wine Spectator* magazine that the California border doesn't start at Eugene. On their map our Illinois Valley didn't exist even though they gave us ratings like Best Buy. ■ TED GERBER

 OPPOSITE: **Fog over the Pinot noir vines of Eric Lemelson's vineyards in Red Hills above Dundee.**

The whole Oregon wine industry is a drop in the bucket compared to California. Oregon makes five percent of the Pinot noir that California produces every year by volume. ■ JESSE LANGE

Even in the early years, the potential was there. Certainly, we've made a lot of mistakes. But we passed laws that really were tough, the toughest in the world. We taxed ourselves at the highest rate in the world so we'd have some money to do some things as an industry. I'm not going to say that we made all the right decisions along the way but we had the right fundamentals and that's why we've been so successful. ■ KEVIN CHAMBERS

For lack of a better term, I call it the Oregon mystique. There is something very special going on here, something that people can only get by coming and visiting Oregon. That's why we do Oregon Pinot Camp where we invite sommeliers and restaurateurs from around the world to Oregon. Afterwards I hear fifty-two different stories about how incredible it is that Oregonians when they make wine are so collaborative and such a big family of friends. They tell us, "Don't lose that. Hang on to that."

I don't think that I could do this any other place. I couldn't do this in California. I couldn't do this in Washington, I couldn't do this in Europe. Because there is something real positive and welcoming about Oregon. It's a friendly environment in which to do this very stressful job. I can't imagine doing this anywhere else. ■ ANNIE SHULL

Chapter 2

The Roots, the Vision

Exactly how those first vines got to Oregon is shrouded in mystery. There's a story about an English sailor stuffing seeds in his boots when he came to the Oregon Coast, to Astoria. And the mission grape—the basis for Mission wine—was already in California.

The mountain men never got very far from alcohol. When they ran out of beaver pelts or got too old to trap for the Hudson's Bay Company at Fort Vancouver, they started farming and planting grapes. Those old French Canadians moved to an area we now call French Prairie to hack out homesteads. This was years before the Oregon Trail, as early as 1823.

In the 1870s and 1880s, when a wine industry was starting to develop here, there were two camps of thought as to what variety to plant in Oregon. One was that American varieties were best because they were very hardy, thick-skinned, and would travel well on railroad cars to the markets in Chicago and New York. So guys like Henderson Luelling, the horticulturist, were encouraging farmers to plant American varieties: Concords and Niagaras. At the same time there were people like Ernest Rueter* at David Hill who said, "This is a great place for premium European varieties. This is a great place to grow cool-climate grapes to make cool-climate wines."

OPPOSITE: Some of the first vintages of post-Prohibition wine can be found in the historic collection in the backroom of Nick's Italian Cafe in downtown McMinnville.

---

*Some references spell the name Reuter.

↵ ABOVE: "Bonded winery number 7" is neatly printed on the front wall of the weathered Adolph H. Doerner winery building in the Umpqua area near Roseburg. The winery was originally started by Adam Doerner, a German immigrant in the 1890s. His son, Adolph, continued the operation. While the winery has ceased production, the Doerner vineyards are still operational.

Notes from the Oregon Horticultural Society reflect both opinions. They eventually came up with lists of varieties that they suggested growing. In those lists under European variety was something called Burgundy and something else called Red Burgundy. It is possible people recognized way back then that the Willamette Valley was a great place to grow Pinot noir. ■ STEPHEN CARY

By 1883, Ernest Rueter had a vineyard right here at this David Hill Winery location. He was making Alsatian wines, such as Pinot blanc, Gewürztraminer, Riesling, and a couple of others. He ran a pretty successful vineyard, shipped wines to Europe, and he even won a gold medal at the 1904 St. Louis World's Fair. Two things happened: First, in 1913, the stevedores siphoned out the wine he was shipping in large casks to Germany and replaced it with water. Of course, it was refused on delivery, and because he didn't have any backup capital, he went broke. And then Oregon went dry in 1914. Rueter tore out his grapes and put in orchards. ■ MILAN STOYANOV

I have photographs from 1911 of Zinfandel vines in The Dalles. It seems they were planted in the late 1800s, by an Italian stone mason named Louie Comini. He came to this area when he heard about the Italians building the Cascade Locks. No one knows if he brought cuttings up out of the San Francisco Bay Area or if he had them sent from Italy. ■ LONNIE WRIGHT

When we first came here to the Umpqua area, we saw these old abandoned Zin vineyards just a mile north of where we are now. In the late 1800s, German-immigrant brothers named Von Pessl came up here from the Beringer Winery in Napa and planted some cuttings. They were in communication

 LEFT: Richard Sommer, founder of Hillcrest winery talks with Dyson DeMara, the winemaker who bought the historic winery near Roseburg in 2003. Sommer started in 1961, making Hillcrest one of Oregon's oldest post-Prohibition vineyards and wineries. (Only Honeywood winery, which started with its fruit wines in the Salem area, has been in continuous operation longer.) Sommer experimented with a variety of grapes, including Pinot noir, even before the modern-era Willamette Valley growers.

with another German named Adam Doerner who worked as a cooper at Beringer. The Von Pessls told Doerner, "We've planted these cuttings, and they're doing really well. You should come up here and grow grapes." So in 1888, Doerner came up with cuttings of Kleinberger, Zinfandel, and some kind of Sauvignon, planted a vineyard, and built a distillery and a commercial winery that did five thousand gallons a year.

So when we asked people if you could grow Zinfandel here, everyone told us that it was too cold in Oregon. But we were looking at all those old Zin vineyards and the remains of Doerner's winery thinking, "God, they had a winery for seventy years. How the hell do you make five thousand gallons of wine without a tractor for a lot of that time?" They had to be busting their ass. But they did it. ■ DYSON DEMARA

Oregon really started out with a bunch of well-educated hippies sitting around in meadows passing around bottles, critiquing each other. They had no bias about sharing information. It was all about sharing information. That spirit is still very much alive today.
■ JOSH BERGSTRÖM

Fortunately for the industry there were some visionary people—someone who can look past the present. Charles Coury was one of them. Richard Sommer down in Roseburg was another. He was really the first to grow vinifera in modern times but gets very little credit for it.

The rest of us, we were all kind of waddling around up here. None of us were farmers. We were all kind of professional people of one sort or another. I was an engineer. Dick Erath was an engineer, Charles Coury was a meteorologist, David Lett sold books. Bringing together all of these talents and interests was really pretty fortunate for Oregon. We were planning the industry. Here was a blank piece of paper. What do we want to do? ■ DICK PONZI

Most people have never heard of Richard Sommer's Hillcrest winery. But Richard was an experimenter extraordinaire. There are around eight thousand grape varieties in the world, and he came up with the varieties that Oregon is known for in one place at one time in the early 1960s when people at UC Davis were saying you couldn't do it in Oregon. He made Pinot blanc, Pinot gris, the whole Cabernet family, Pinot noir, Riesling, Sauvignon blanc, and Gewürztraminer. ■ DYSON DEMARA

I got the original cuttings from Louie (spelled Louis) Martini Vineyard in Napa and planted in April of 1961. I learned as I went. After I started making wine, people came out of the woodwork to buy it. At the beginning, they were just the local people. And some of them would say: "Yeah, it's pretty good wine,

LEFT: With the spirit of exploration still burning strong, Dick and Nancy Ponzi stand in their newly planted olive orchard. They are also experimenting with new grape varietals. Dick came with an engineering background when he and Nancy planted their first Pinot noir vines in the Willamette Valley and founded Ponzi Vineyards in 1970. RIGHT: Located in a farmhouse built in 1883, David Hill Winery has lots of history. First, Ernest Rueter had a vineyard and made wine here in the late 1800s. Then Charles Coury, a post-Prohibition pioneer, started growing vines and making wine here in the 1960s. The winery is near Forest Grove in the northern Willamette Valley.

RIGHT: Green Pinot noir grape vines slope up to the Domaine Drouhin Winery near Dundee, Oregon. Many consider French winemaker Robert Drouhin's decision to buy land, plant a vineyard, and build a winery in the Willamette Valley as a pivotal moment in Oregon's wine history. It was a recognition of the Willamette Valley as a world class place to grow Pinot noir.

BELOW: Dick Erath, one of the first to plant vineyards and start a winery in the Willamette Valley, has since sold his Erath brand. He has, however, retained his Oregon vineyards and has planted new vines in Arizona.

Richard, but it's kind of sour. You got anything sweeter?" I heard that litany for many a moon, so I started making a blend called Mellow Red. I took Riesling, added Zinfandel for color, and sweetened it with sugar. ■ RICHARD SOMMER

When I was living in Walnut Creek in California, I took a course at UC Davis about making wine. I asked one of the professors, Vern Singleton, what's going on in the Pacific Northwest? He told me, "Talk to the guy in the back of the classroom there. He's from Oregon." It was Richard Sommer from Roseburg, and he couldn't wait to give me a bottle of wine that he had made.

When I got home, I pulled out the cork, poured the wine, and it just smelled like whiskey. It was a Cabernet that he had made. But he didn't have much money so he was getting freshly emptied whiskey barrels from Hood River Distillery. He didn't even bother to wash them out because he wanted to get that extra little hit from the

whiskey; so the wine went right in. Of course, it smelled like whiskey, but behind all that there was some nice fruit character there. ■ DICK ERATH

In 1968, Dick Erath came up my driveway. He had this old, beat up BMW and this big old beard, and this sheath of paper underneath his arm. He said, "I'm Dick Erath, I've looked all over the west coast for a great viticulture site, and I think you're sitting on it. Do you want to try something new?" At the time, I was actually kind of desperate because I was sitting on several hundred tons of unsold prunes.

Well, I was thinking anything would be better than forty-dollar-a-ton prunes. I said, "Okay, Dick, I'll tell you what, we'll plant an acre and a half of Riesling and an acre of Pinot noir, but I'm going to need a lot of help on this thing. I know how to grow good fruit but I don't know how to grow wine grapes." He assured me that he had all this knowledge and knew exactly what to do.

We put on our first vineyard in 1970, and then had our first crush in 1973. Our first wine wasn't really great, but it showed potential. ■ JIM AND MARTHA MARESH

Dick Erath had a celebration at his house for his twenty-fifth crush. There were about two hundred people and we're drinking this great Oregon Pinot. Dick and I were sitting under a tree, and he said to me, "Jim, did you ever think it would be this big?"

I said, "No."

He said, "Back in 1970, we sure didn't know what we were doing."

I said, "You told me right in front of your crusher you knew what you were doing; now twenty-five years later, after I had pulled out all my orchard, you tell me different?"

And he said, "I didn't have a clue." ■ JIM MARESH

∽ ABOVE: Jim Maresh, a businessman and naval officer turned farmer, pulled out most of his prune, cherry, and hazelnut orchards in the 1970s to plant vineyards in the Red Hills above Dundee upon Dick Erath's suggestion. Here he stands in front of his Sauvignon blanc vines. NEXT PAGE: In the Willamette Valley near Dayton, a shaft of light streaks across Stoller's hillside vineyard behind an old metal barn in the foreground.

When I was working as an engineer at Cal Tech in California, I went on a vacation and by chance discovered Oregon's first winery, Hillcrest Vineyard out of Roseburg. After tasting the wine and talking with the winemaker, I discovered the potential was great there. "Boy it looks like a good wine region," I thought to myself. I decided to quit the rat race in California, moved to southern Oregon, started growing grapes and making some wine in 1971. ■ PHILIPPE GIRARDET

We were two liberal arts graduates; we had no farming or business training; we chose to grow a grape, Pinot noir, that had never done well in the United States; and we decided to grow this grape in Oregon, which had no wine industry. It was the kind of decision that you make when you're young, you don't know what you're getting into, you're willing to risk everything, you have energy, and you're willing to substitute your time for money. ■ SUSAN SOKOL BLOSSER

While I was winemaker at Sokol Blosser, the Oregon Department of Agriculture had this dairy mentality, the idea of cleanliness being next to godliness. We had one inspector who vowed he would get barrels out of the cellar because you can't pour wine in wood. It's just not clean. ■ BOB MCRITCHIE, PH.D.

There was a whole lot of ignorance at the time. I remember going to the London Grill at the Benson for dinner one time. It was probably our first or second year growing grapes, so that was in the early 1970s. When we explained that we had just planted a small vineyard, the waiter said, "No, you can't grow European varieties here because the minute you put them in the soil, they're going to revert back to the American variety." ■ PAT CAMBPELL

The first time I marketed wine in New York in late 1978, I had to carry a map of Oregon to show people where Oree-gone was. You know that's how it's pronounced back there. ■ BILL BLOSSER

↪ ABOVE: Bill Blosser and Susan Sokol Blosser planted their first vines in 1971 and built one of Oregon's first tasting rooms in 1978. Today they have left most of the day-to-day winery operations to their children, Alex and Allison Sokol Blosser.
BELOW: Pat Campbell (right) reminisces with son Adam about some of the rougher times during the transition of Elk Cove winery.

In those early years there was this belief in the Whole Earth catalogue concept that you could learn anything, you just needed the right book.

When we started in 1971, it was a pretty special time in America. It was a continuation of the 1960s in terms of the freedom. People were given permission to do something that they wanted to do rather than what they had studied or what their parents did. There was a huge generational shift. Many vineyards and wineries all around America trace their roots back to that period, because the people who were starting them came from families whose parents didn't drink wine and for whom wine was not important. But this new generation had been exposed to wine typically by being in Europe. That was certainly our case. I'd spent a year there as a junior and my wife at that time, Ginny, and I spent the summer of 1969 in Europe getting entranced with food, wine, and the relationship between them.

We wanted to move out to the country but not be too far from Portland. When we came over the Chehalem Mountains, we felt that this was a special place, somehow related to Europe. Obviously we were influenced by fantasy, not necessarily reality.

We heard from a realtor that somebody had planted grapes in the area. As we drove along Kings Grade Road, we came upon this big guy with a wheelbarrow and a beard. Something made us stop to ask him if he knew anyone who had planted grapes. He turned around and said that he actually did know someone that had planted grapes. He pointed to his vineyard. That was Dick Erath. Later we met Bill Blosser, who introduced us to David Lett. After a month or two, we knew everybody in the Oregon wine business. ■ DAVID ADELSHEIM

LEFT: Dave Adelsheim started the winery with his then-wife, Ginny, in 1971, not so much as a business, but rather a lifestyle change. He recalls that they, like most of the other early wine pioneers, worked at other jobs to support their need to grow grapes and make wine. RIGHT: David Lett, considered by many to be the first to plant Pinot noir in the Willamette Valley in the post-Prohibition era, tastes just-harvested fruit from the South Block at The Eyrie Vineyards Winery in McMinnville, Yamhill County. This is the vineyard producing the wines that placed well in competitions against French Burgundies in the 1970s.

Definitely, the most incredible moment for me was after we placed in the Drouhin tasting in 1980. That was the blind tasting in Beaune, France. The first tasting, the year before, where we placed, I didn't even know that we had entered. My distributor did it. But when we came in second in Drouhin's competition that really made us. For Pete's sake, that made all the damn peasants out here in Oregon, who didn't believe we were world class, take a look at us. ■ DAVID LETT

After I had tasted David Lett's and Dick Erath's wines, I felt that David's wines were a little too light, there wasn't enough there. Whereas, Erath's early wines had a lot there, but they tended to be very soft and lacked acidity and structure. I wanted to take the skeleton that Lett did really nicely, sort of a Twiggy wine, and combine with—who is the country singer with the big boobs—yea, Dolly Parton. So I wanted to combine it with Erath's voluptuous Dolly Parton kind of wines. I wanted to make a Meryl Streep sort of thing in the middle. ■ MYRON REDFORD

↩ ABOVE: Myron Redford, owner of Amity Vineyards, during harvest.

I think the big breakthrough was Domaine Drouhin coming here. I remember one time they had invited the winemakers and a few vineyard people like myself to their first barrel tasting. I was standing next to Dick Erath, tasting this stuff right out of the barrel. I said: "God, this stuff is good, Dick, could you do this?" He said: "If I had three million dollars I could do it." And that kind of told a story of the fact that we were so blessed to have survived as long as we did, until the next wave of people came with not only knowledge, but also the capital to take the whole Oregon wine scene to the next level. ■ JIM MARESH

ᔭ ABOVE: David Lett
discusses Pinot noir from
the famous South Block
vineyard with son Jason Lett,
the current winemaker at
The Eyrie Vineyards Winery
in McMinnville.

In the early 1980s, when I was a very young lobbyist for the National Federation
of Independent Business, Richard Sommer and Scott Henry, who developed
the Scott Henry trellis system, were members. They called wanting help with
legislation to grow the industry. Scott Henry, especially, was always a business
builder. It's kind of interesting that the industry now is very heavily weighted
in the North Willamette, but really a lot of the early leadership had to do with
those down in the Umpqua. ▪ JIM BERNAU

One problem was that we had two organizations: the Oregon Wine Growers
Association in Roseburg and the Oregon Wine Council up here. And the people here didn't like the people there because the people there were more social
and up here they wanted to be more technical. But the legislators didn't want
to sponsor any bills until we had one organization representing the whole

~ Lᴇꜰᴛ: Winemaker and owner, Harry Peterson-Nedry (right) checks the color of a Pinot noir with a flashlight with co-winemaker Mike Eyres at Chehalem Winery near Newberg, Willamette Valley. Aʙᴏᴠᴇ: Cecil Zerba of Zerba Cellars holds cuttings that he started at his winery near Milton-Freewater in the Walla Walla AVA of Oregon.

state. We worked all day in the meeting room of a restaurant in Albany until everybody was in agreement. We liked their name better than our name, so that wasn't an issue. Then we had a lawyer who was a grape grower put it in writing. ■ BILL FULLER

When I was growing up in the 1970s and 1980s, there wasn't anybody else in school whose parents were doing anything involved with wine. While agriculture was a big part of the local school culture, grape growing back then was just something totally weird and not necessarily respected like it is today. Kids would say, "Oh, that's pretty crazy. Why are you doing that here?" It's a real contrast to today where I think schools in Yamhill, in a class of twenty kids, there might be five, six kids whose parents are somehow involved in this industry. ■ ADAM CAMPBELL

In Oregon winemaking, the Steamboat Conference was one of the biggest contributors. Started in 1979 by Steve Cary, winemaker at Yamhill Valley, and a few other people, it brought together winemakers from California, Oregon, and eventually the rest of the world to share their insights, their mistakes, their new discoveries. ■ DAVID ADELSHEIM

The Oregon wine business has gone through various phases or waves of growth. Starting in the mid to late sixties, the industry was set up by pioneers who had technical backgrounds, who were somewhat obstinate and who sought to do things that other people couldn't do. In many instances they are still pretty obstinate individuals.

Following those pioneers was a phase of romantics, people who didn't know how to do it, but knew they wanted to do it. I arrived in 1980, very much a part of this second wave.

The next wave was full of people who had some resources, so this might be the doctor's phase or the owners-of-business' phase.

There's also an apprentice wave, people who came here for a job and they were passionate about wine, but in the beginning they couldn't afford to plant

~ Aʙᴏᴠᴇ: Bill Fuller was Oregon's only modern-era wine pioneer who came with real winemaking experience—nine years as a winemaker in Napa Valley, a degree in Chemistry, and a degree in Enology. In fact, Fuller recalls that it was in his yard in St. Helena, California, where David Lett made his first cuttings before bringing them to the Willamette Valley. Bill actually ended up in Oregon because his pregnant wife didn't want to move to Bill's original choice of California's Anderson Valley. Bill and investor Bill Malkmus founded Tualatin Estate Vineyards in 1973.

RIGHT: Winemaker Rollin Soles spent part of his junior year of college working in a vineyard in Switzerland. After meeting winemakers from France, Italy, and Germany, he decided he was going to make wine. He then went to work in Australia before becoming the winemaker at Argyle in Dundee.

their own grapes or start their own winery. After five, ten, maybe twenty years, they established their own dream winery. ■ HARRY PETERSON-NEDRY

When we were living in Santa Barbara at the time, we got these two wines, drank them and said, "ooh man, they had the goods." The wines were a 1980 Eyrie and a 1979 Maresh Vineyard/Erath. Erath's phone number was right on the label and you know we drank that bottle and called Dick Erath. We just called him up out of the blue and he came to the phone and was very friendly and engaging, and he said "yeah, come on up." At the time, we were still approaching things from a California perspective. We thought, "Oh wow, it's way up there in the frozen north, right next to Alaska where the glaciers had just retreated." When we got to Dundee, it was like "eureka!"; it really is here that we wanted to do wine. ■ DON AND WENDY LANGE

I was working Chateau La Tour Blanche, a school for techniques of viticulture and enology, when out of the blue I got a call from Lelo and Bob Kerivan. I don't know why he called the school, but the director just said, "You've been to the United States, pick up this phone call. Somebody wants to hire a winemaker in the United States." Bob pretty much hired me over the phone. We hit it off and I started as a winemaker at Bridgeview in southern Oregon in 1988.

What a great opportunity. I was only twenty-four years old and Bob listened to everything I had to say and implemented as much as he could. Then I met Bernie LaCroute and started working at WillaKenzie in 1995. Bernie pretty much told me, "The sky's the limit; let's do everything the best way we can." So I designed the winery and the whole shebang there. It was a lot of fun. Now I have my own winery.
■ LAURENT MONTALIEU

LEFT: Laurent Montalieu checks the temperature of fermenting wine at his own winery, Solena, in McMinnville. Originally from France, Laurent came to the United States as a winemaker for Bridgeview Vineyard and Winery in southern Oregon, then moved to WillaKenzie Estate Winery before founding his own operation.

There was an ad in Sue Horstmann and Willamette Valley Wineries Association's bulletin from a guy who wanted to buy a winery. So just out of curiosity, I called him up. He was very honest, "Oh, this is an ego winery." The guy wanted to buy a winery. He didn't care whether the brand was established, all he wanted was a small facility with a small vineyard so that he could hire a winemaker and make wine. He just wanted to be part of the wine scene. ■ MYRON REDFORD

We had been traveling to wine regions around the world and found the grape we loved in Burgundy. Then it was just deciding where we wanted to establish the winery. We live in Minnesota, but we could have done it anywhere in the world. When we tasted some Pinot noir from Oregon, we weren't impressed with the wine, but the fruit was luscious. We knew that is where we needed to go; Oregon was the place of all the places in the world. At that point we had

never been in Oregon, but since we wanted to grow great Pinot noir, it needed to be in the Dundee Hills.

We started Domaine Serene in 1989, and produced our first wine in 1990. Even that first year, Parker scored one of our wines a 90. We knew we were on the right track. ■ GRACE EVENSTAD

I spent my whole career in the wholesale lumber business and ended up running a company in Portland. My wife and I used to come out here to David Hill, as well as a lot of other wineries, to taste and buy wine. When we came out here in 1992, there was a for sale sign out here.

The place was falling down; it hadn't been well taken care of for a long time. And I don't know, we bought it from our heart, certainly not as an investment. At that moment I was seven or eight years away from retirement, and as I got closer I figured my golf game was too bad to play golf five days a week. And I really wanted to keep my hand in business.

I said, "God I'd really like to be responsible for fixing that up." And I looked at the vineyards and I said, "I'd really like to be responsible for improving them." So we bought the place. ■ MILAN STOYANOV

☙ ABOVE: A panorama view of the Knudsen and Bella Vida vineyards and the surrounding Red Hills of Dundee. Just barely visible to the right is Erath Winery.

I think there are lots of elements of that original culture left. Look at the new people coming in, particularly those who come without large amounts of money. They come with passion, excitement, and desire to learn about wine, particularly Oregon wine. They also know that they get to stand on the shoulders of the people that came before them, but nonetheless are willing to get dirty and really make a contribution to the industry. It's much tougher, though, to make that place for yourself today than it was when I started. The bar is so high; nobody's going to get in the business in the north Willamette Valley with the goal to make a fifteen-dollar Pinot noir.
■ DAVID ADELSHEIM

As a small ma-and-pa operation I still have a day job, half time. Monday, Tuesday, Wednesday I work the day job. But during the growing season here in the Willamette Valley it stays light out until 9:30, so I can come home from

ABOVE LEFT: Ed King III in his office at King Estate Winery at the south end of the Willamette Valley. It seems that Ed went to buy hay from a farm near Lorane but ended up buying the whole farm instead. The mud on his shoes shows that he gets out in the vineyard.
ABOVE RIGHT: Owner and winemaker Joe Dobbes rolling a portable humidifier in his Wine by Joe facility in Dundee, Willamette Valley.

↶ LEFT: Winemaker and owner Patty Green with stir rod in French oak barrels at Patricia Green Cellars, Ribbon Ridge AVA, Willamette Valley. She started picking grapes at historic Hillcrest Winery near Roseburg and eventually became the winemaker. From there she continued winemaking at a string of other wineries until she started Patricia Green Cellars.

work and I can get in a spray or mow after work and still have light to see. After fourteen years, I'm finally drawing compensation from the company. ■ SCOTT SHULL

Obviously I grew up here, and since about 1993, I started blending wine with Dad. Then in 1996, Dad left on vacation right during harvest. He left it up to me. I remember feeling a little like I was bluffing it a bit, like I was learning as I went. It hasn't been until the last five or six years that I've felt like I really know what I'm doing. Believe it or not, I'm not pretending anymore. ■ LUISA PONZI

Luisa's style and my style are pretty close. In fact, I have to say she's a little more sophisticated, a little more of a delicate touch. But the most rewarding thing for me was the times when we sat down together to taste the blends. At the beginning, I would formulate the batches. The next year I would be less

RIGHT: Dick Ponzi, one of Oregon's modern-era pioneer winegrowers, receives some wine from his daughter and wine-maker Luisa Ponzi at Ponzi Vineyards winery.

influential. Over a four-year period I was out of the picture. It was, I've never told this to anybody, but it's like I didn't need to be there any more. But I really enjoyed being a part of that transition. I've surrendered it to her completely. ■ DICK PONZI

I was fired quite a few times. But they were very short firings. By the end of the day I think that they realized, and I realized, that our conflict was only about wanting to make this place great; you can't fault the other person for just wanting to do a great job and make a great product. ■ ADAM CAMPBELL

My greatest motivation in succeeding is that my dad put his entire retirement into this thing. It can't fail. That's a lot to live up to. My parent's whole life, everything they own is tied up in this business. If that isn't motivation to succeed I don't know what is. ■ JOSH BERGSTRÖM

I worked in the vineyard growing up. But I wanted to leave pretty much from the time I graduated high school.

෴ LEFT: Winemaker Terry Casteel with his winemaker son, Ben, in the barrel room at Bethel Heights Vineyard winery, Eola Hills, Willamette Valley. Since Parkinson's disease has dramatically affected Terry's ability to smell, he is proud to have Ben step in to fill the winemaker shoes.

Then Dad asked me to come back. This was the first time he said, "I want you to come here to work, manage the vineyards and make the wine." This was a huge, huge step. I couldn't say no. There is also a matter of his health; it doesn't seem to be getting worse but it doesn't seem to be getting better either. I wanted to be here to help with that too. If he were still in perfect health, I would have said no because he just loves this work too much. Eyrie has been his job, his hobby, his mistress, his sports car, his midlife crisis, and then his late life crisis. It's part of his blood.

Well, it's not easy; but on the other hand I felt when I came back that this was my opportunity to have a conversation with Dad. If I didn't have that conver-sation now, I'll always wish I had taken that opportunity. That's partly why I'm here. Now I am part of Oregon history. And that's a burden and blessing.
■ JASON LETT

Chapter 3

The Terroir

It's not just the slope of the land; it's not just the way the sun hits the hillside; it's not just the depth of the soil, the nutrients in the soil, and the kind of soil; it's not just the climate. Rather it's the fog, the rain, the Indian summer, and our Jory, Willakenzie, and Laurelwood soils. It's the big oaks, the native oaks, the big leaf maples, the lavender, the insects, the bees, the bluebirds, and the swallows. It's all these things coming together in one place that make it just right. ■ SUSAN SOKOL BLOSSER

I think we will find some nuances here in Oregon, but it takes time. It's only one harvest a year, so it's a very slow experience, but we can already see that the Dundee Hills tend to give wine of a lighter texture—not so big, not so tannic. A little bit farther south, the Eola Hills produce a more spicy, more colorful wine. We still have to discover the nuances. It's very slow and it takes time to learn. So we keep notes on everything, every year—the wines, the blocks. And hopefully the next generation, or those who comes after them, will continue. That's how you build, you learn. ■ VÉRONIQUE DROUHIN-BOSS

Southern Oregon has the luxury of many microclimates and the ability to do a wide variety of grapes and wines very well, whereas the Willamette Valley focuses primarily on its Pinot noir. It is both a blessing and a burden to have the ability to grow a wide variety of grapes and to make a wide variety of

〜 OPPOSITE: Storm clouds and streaks of light sail across the landscape and vineyard planted by Cecil Zerba on the old Cockburn farm near Milton-Freewater in the Walla Walla AVA.

wines; we don't have that single varietal focus that the Willamette Valley has so we are a little bit scattered in our approach to marketing in that respect. ■ LAURA LOTSPEICH

ↀ **OPPOSITE: Dry bare rolling hills surround the Seven Hills Vineyard in the Walla Walla AVA near Milton-Freewater. Norm McKibben, one of the partners has experimented with various irrigation techniques to maximize water usage. He is a firm believer of sustainable viticulture.**

The Eola Hills have rich volcanic soils that influence the flavor of Bethel Heights wine. But two blocks of land, separated by twenty feet, turn out very different Pinot noirs. The Flat Block consistently produces an elegant seductive wine that emphasizes purity of fruit and delicacy of character. The Southeast Block is a powerful, masculine wine with a rich, spicy component that can knock your socks off—same clone of Pinot noir, same winemaker, same procedure. The difference is only twenty feet. Some French soil scientists told us that the blocks were probably formed by separate volcanic events. That's terroir. ■ TERRY CASTEEL

More than 200 million years ago Oregon's coastline was near the Idaho border. The western half of Oregon did not exist. Washington State did not exist. Over the subsequent 200 million years the Juan de Fuca Plate collided with the North America Continental Plate. The Juan de Fuca Plate plunges underneath the coastline. As it does, the mother rock of the plate plunges down at about a forty-five degree angle, shearing off soft sediments of the ocean floor. As this happens, soil is pillowed and added to the coastline.

Just 20 million years ago there was an incredibly violent chain of volcanoes on the far eastern Oregon border, including the Blue Mountains. This was the greatest event of its kind on the planet. It released enough basalt to raise the elevation of Bend twenty-five hundred feet. These eruptions are called the Columbia River Basalt Flows. No other event on earth has issued this much material. ■ KEN WRIGHT

Here in Oregon you have two basic soil types: those derived from volcanic sources and those derived from sedimentary sources. Then within those two basic derivations there are umpteen doodle numbers of conditions: deeper

soils, shallower soils, rockier soils, less rocky soils, more acidic, less acidic—
many different permutations. ■ ROLLIN SOLES

We call the two basic Willamette Valley soil types Jory and Willakenzie. Jory
was created from the massive volcanic flows from eastern Oregon which
formed every one of the headlands along the Oregon Coast—Cascade Head,
Tillamook Head, Cape Lookout—as well as the Eola Hills, Salem Hills,
Dundee Hills, Parrot's Mountain, and Pete's Mountain. They are fourteen to
sixteen million-year-old Columbia Basalts, which have been weathering ever
since that time, forming nice, red soils low in nutrients.

The Willakenzie soil, on the west side of Yamhill and Washington coun-
ties, contains sediments from the bottom of the ocean brought up by the col-
lision of the Juan de Fuca Plate and Continental Plate forming the Coast
Range mountains.

Both soils look the same in the field. They're both old, red, and have clay.
When somebody pours me a glass of Pinot noir from the Willamette Valley,
I can tell if the grapes were grown in the Jory soil on basalt bedrock, or in
Willakenzie soil on the marine sediments. ■ SCOTT BURNS, PH.D.

Jory is Oregon's most famous soil designation. There was even an ill-conceived
effort in the legislature to make it the state soil. The name comes from the Jory
family, who homesteaded in the South Salem hills, just about three miles due
west from here. And there's a cemetery of their family just a short distance
from here. ■ JIM BERNAU

At the end of the last glacial period, an ice dam formed cutting off the Clark
Fork River, which drained western Montana. The melting glaciers formed a
lake that was 2,000 feet deep and over 250 cubic miles of water.

Between 15,000 and 18,000 years ago, in an event known as the Missoula
Floods, the lake was catastrophically released in three days, and all that ice trav-
eled sixty miles an hour down through Spokane and across eastern Washington,
carving out the coulees and carrying silt across Walla Walla and down the

↬ LEFT: **Sunrise over Elk Cove Vineyard winery's Five Mountain Vineyard in Washington County with Mt. Hood in the misty background.**

Columbia River into Portland. The rushing water carved out Lake Oswego, filled the Tualatin and Willamette valleys to four hundred foot elevation, all the way to Eugene. Forty of these floods reached Oregon. Those floods deposited all that silt in the valley bottoms. Down in Dayton and Newberg, you've got Missoula Flood sediments that are 150 feet thick; as you get down to Eugene it's only a couple of feet thick. All of this silt is too rich in nutrients to produce great wine grapes. ■ SCOTT BURNS, PH.D.

I can grow the same grape in two different parts of our vineyard, and I get a different grape. It tastes different. Why, I don't know. We had a vineyard of Pinot that we planted next to the road called the Road Block. We had that vineyard in Pinot for twelve or thirteen years, but never got a good Pinot out of it. So we've pulled it out and replaced it with something else. Whereas on the top of the hill, where we first planted, we've consistently got very good Pinot. Those blocks are two thousand yards apart. I can't explain it. ■ BILL BLOSSER

ꙮ ABOVE: The surrounding landscape and photographer can be seen in the water drops on this Pinot noir grape. RIGHT: The walls of the Columbia River Gorge at Crown Point offer a dramatic view of geologic events in Oregon. The huge basalt flows from eastern Oregon are clearly visible in the walls, but like an iceberg, two-thirds of the basalt is below ground level. The repeated Missoula Floods carved out the Gorge itself.

east side, that's desert, less than ten inches of rain a year. The mountain range behind us blocks a lot of that bad weather. When we're 85 degress here in the summer, it can be 104 in Medford. When it drops to fifty degrees here at night, it might be eighty at night in Medford. ■ DYSON DEMARA

In Oregon, we have the poison oak hypothesis. Since poison oak loves to grow on south-facing slopes at three hundred to eight hundred feet in elevation, I tell people if you're going to buy a piece of property for a vineyard, the first question to ask, "Is there poison oak on the property?" If they say yes, then you're looking in the right direction, because poison oak likes a south-facing slope, which is very dry. ■ SCOTT BURNS, PH.D.

If you're going to plant a grape you've got to match the maturity of the fruit to the area. We have the most natural thing here in our part of the Willamette. We have long days, longer than California's. During those long warm days of spring and summer the plant is pumping out all kinds of energy.

But with the shorter days of fall, as the sun starts going south, the plant senses the end of the season and begins putting energy into the grapes. It wants to ripen the fruit to propagate, to survive as a breed. With the cooler days and evenings, the maturation slows down, allowing the grapes to develop flavors. The peak of ripeness happens right before the harvest. If you pick too early, you lose that opportunity.

In warm areas the fruit ripens at the time of the highest temperatures. That's bad. The fruit just goes crazy in terms of ripening, because the metabolism is activated in a more rapid way. ■ DICK AND NANCY PONZI

All of the grape varietals that grow in the Willamette are cool climate varietals. Yet they're ripening when the leaves on the trees are changing color, when the animals that migrate are migrating, the animals that hibernate are hibernating, and there's not enough sunlight and heat to further ripen the tomatoes and apples and grapes. In Oregon, Pinot noir, Chardonnay, and Riesling

ᴖ Opposite: **Morning fog rises from the Willamette Valley below the Pinot gris vines at Elk Cove Vineyard winery's Five Mountain Vineyard.**

ᓚ RIGHT: Workers harvest part of the 210 acres of vines at Del Rio Vineyards and Winery in the Rogue Valley appellation of southern Oregon. Located between the Cascade and Siskiyou mountain ranges, the site was orginally a stage coach stop, then transformed to a pear orchard in the 1920s and in the late 1990s became a vineyard. OPPOSITE: Sunrise over Weisinger's vineyard in the Rogue Valley of southern Oregon near Ashland. John Weisinger started planting the vineyards in 1979, then built his winery and tasting room in 1988.

ripen at the end of the growing season. This gives the most vibrancy in the fruit and in the wine. ■ ROLLIN SOLES

Here in the northern Willamette Valley, the Van Duzer Corridor is a low point in the coast range that lets the ocean breezes come in during the afternoon. The Eola Hills are closer to it than the Red Hills. About four o'clock in the afternoon we begin to get a sea breeze that cools things off rather dramatically. This means that the wines have more acidity, not necessarily more sugar, and the balance is a little different. ■ TERRY CASTEEL

Our rainfall is closer to California's than it is to Burgundy's in terms of pattern. They have summer rain and we have summer drought. California usually has more sun than Oregon, except in the month of July. Burgundy is basically tracking with Oregon up through June, when Oregon suddenly has much more sun. We also have clearer, less rainy summer days than Burgundy. That spike in sunlight, and the fact that Oregon overtakes Burgundy in terms

of heat at the end of the growing season, despite it being cooler the rest of the growing season, is the reason we have more fruitiness in our wine than they do. ■ DAVID ADELSHEIM

People ask why are Oregon vineyards planted on hills? When a cold front moves through, those hills drain the cold air off. To protect the vines from frost, they have to be on a slope where the cold air is shed down the slope.

You actually get a little bit of heat from the friction of the moving air that prevents frost damage. Where the cold settles on the valley floor you may lose a crop every two or three years. ■ JIM KAKACEK

The vintages recently have been more on the warm side. But, I'd have to admit, it makes things a lot easier. This dry, warm weather eliminates worrying about when to harvest. You've got a bigger window for harvesting now than we ever had before. Some of us old-timers joke when the newer wineries that have come in the last ten to fifteen years see rain in October or September, they freak out. That was a normal occurrence for us, because we were picking in October and November, and those November periods were always threatened by rain. Yet some of the recent cooler vintages—1996 and 1995—those really wet years, produced some of the better wines. ■ DICK AND NANCY PONZI

I think global warming will determine what will be planted in the future. We've already seen it. Our harvests are now at least two weeks, many times a month earlier than in the seventies when we started. Some of that could be normal changes in weather patterns. But if it continues, studies show that some of the prime vineyards in California are not going to be suited for growing grapes like Cabernet. And there will be a lot of areas in Oregon where Cabernet will do really well where it doesn't do so well now. We might see those big changes over the next twenty, thirty years. ■ BILL BLOSSER

ঝ OPPOSITE: Sunrise over the vineyards and tasting room of Melrose Vineyards Winery near Roseburg, in the Umpqua area. Wayne and Deedy Parker created Melrose Vineyards in 1996.

ঝ 67

Chapter 4

The Vineyard

The vines just want to have babies. They don't care about wine. That's our problem. And the part we make into wine is nourishment to the seed to make the babies. If they sense that it is a terrible place to have babies because of the weather or because of their health, then they'll abort and we'll have very little crop. But if they sense that it's sunny and everything is happy, they'll pour it on and have more babies. But they don't have the same standards we do. We have to get up to 20 to 24 percent sugar. They don't. If they put on too many grapes, we can't ripen those to our standards. ■ ALLEN HOLSTEIN

In twenty-five years, and I will tell you which areas are best: from trial and error, from making wines, from putting in different clones of Pinot noir, and from learning how to manage the land. The more you know your land, the better you are going to do. You may prune differently, you may change your trellis system, and you may do things differently all based on the knowledge you gain from working on that piece of land. ■ BERNARD LACROUTE

I don't know one thing in a vineyard that we do today that we did back when we first planted in 1972. ■ DAVID ADELSHEIM

ᔕ OPPOSITE: Fresh spring snow falls on Bella Vida and Maresh vineyards with Maresh's Red Barn tasting room in the background in the Red Hills above Dundee, Willamette Valley.

Vineyards are kind of a masochistic thing here in Oregon. We put ourselves through a lot of stress. When you think about it, this is a pretty ridiculous industry. We have millions of dollars of investments that all depend on whether it rains or not. ■ JOSH BERGSTRÖM

S o what's a year in the vineyard look like? September and October is harvest. The earliest we ever started in the Willamette was August 30 in 1992. The latest was probably October 20. As harvest starts, it gets busier and busier and more chaotic. Then it's just out of control. You get conflicting instructions, equipment breaking down, and changing weather forecasts. You just react. You don't really think long term or plan. At some point you get spit out the other end.

After harvest the vines go to sleep. Maybe there's a flush in root growth around the time of the first rains, but they've been working hard so they're going into a rest period.

November–March is the time to organize next years' plantings. We put in trellis, and if it's dry enough, we actually plant new vines. A lot of the strategy is to take the highs and lows out of the work level. We keep people busy because they have to eat twelve months out of the year even if there's not work for twelve months. We start pruning around Thanksgiving; it's a little bit earlier than a lot of people do it, but pruning takes all the way until March.

Mid-April buds begin to break. The grapes begin to grow vegetatively before they flower, unlike fruit trees, which flower first.

In late May through July 4, we begin working the foliage wires. Since our rows are close enough together, we lift up wires on opposite sides of a row to force the vines to grow vertically so we can drive a tractor through the rows.

In the middle of June, the big event is flowering. We go out on bloom patrols because it's an important date to note. It is usually one hundred days from bloom to harvest. In the middle of summer when people ask when harvest will be, I'll say, "Well, bloom was on June 15, so harvest will be September 28."

◆ RIGHT: **Phillipe (left) and Jesus from Advanced Vineyard Systems take a break from planting a new Pinot noir vineyard near Newberg, Willamette Valley.**

ᕰ ABOVE TOP: Close-up of leaves and tendrils of vines at Anne Amie Vineyard in Willamette Valley near Lafayette. ABOVE: Blossoms on Chardonnay vines at Domaine Drouhin winery in Willamette Valley near Dundee. RIGHT: Mustards blooming in the Bella Vida and Maresh vineyards in Red Hills above Dundee.

What happens during bloom is a very sexy story. The vineyard has a sweet floral smell, but to actually see the flowers you have to get down with your head under the leaves in the morning light. They cross-pollinate from one flower to the next, rather than self-pollinate, and they don't need insects for help. Pollination of a single female flower can happen multiple times. If there are three seeds in a berry that means there were three fertilizations.

During the summer, I spend a lot of time estimating crops. We go through all the fields and count clusters to come up with an average. When it comes down to short strokes, people will use those numbers at harvest time. All of the sudden when it gets busy, "Okay, we're going to get this field, how many tons are there?" This affects what tank they put it in, and whether or not it all fits in one tank. Then how many people do we need to pick that field? If you have a higher yield than what's estimated, those mistakes compound over the course of a harvest. The goal is to have the whole vineyard picked and every tank and barrel full. ■ ALLEN HOLSTEIN

A tiny louse called phylloxera wiped out many early vineyards that were on their own roots. Now everybody's gone to grafted roots that are resistant to the bug. One year I had a phylloxera problem in a Pinot gris block. About six or eight plants were beginning to fail. I was told: "It's going to wipe out that vineyard, you're going to have to pull it all out."

Well, the people who were leasing the vineyard wanted to stress their vines because then you produce better wine. I never like to stress a plant, because it's like stressing a body, you get sick, you die. So I terminated the lease, and began farming it the way I would farm my cherries, my hazelnuts, my walnuts, and my prunes, where I mulch in the summertime to maintain the moisture. Gradually I restored vigor back into the vines that were infected. Right now when you can walk through that vineyard, you can't find a single sick plant. You've got to keep that plant healthy; at least that's my strategy. ■ JIM MARESH

It takes a lot of hand labor to grow grapes on these hillsides. You can't easily mechanize it. We do over three thinning passes to adjust the crop level. If

ꝏ OPPOSITE: Fall-colored patchwork of Abacela Winery vineyard in the Umpqua region of southern Oregon. ABOVE: Burlap coffee bags used for weed control in the vineyard at Witness Tree Vineyard & Winery near Salem, Willamette Valley. The vineyard takes its name from an ancient oak tree used as a surveyor's landmark in 1854, during the Oregon Trail era.

CLOCKWISE FROM TOP LEFT:
1) Winemaker at Archery Summit Winery, Anna Metzinger, tests the sugar content of some Pinot noir grapes with a refractometer in the vineyards near Dundee, Willamette Valley. 2) Picker holding harvested Cabernet Sauvignon at Seven Hills Vineyard, Walla Walla AVA near Milton Freewater, eastern Oregon. 3) Woman harvester with Cabernet Sauvignon waiting to dump her bucket at Seven Hills Vineyard. 4) Picker harvesting grapes from Bruckmeiers South Fork Vineyard for Melrose Winery near Roseburg, Umpqua AVA. 5) Woman carrying cuttings for planting from executive vineyard manager Allen Holstein's own vineyard above Dundee, Willamette Valley. These cuttings will be planted either in the fall or spring as new vines. 6) Picker harvesting Pinot gris in Henry Estate Winery vineyards near town of Umpqua.

you're in a warm climate on the valley floor, you can use lots of mechanization. They could probably grow grapes for a third of the cost of what we do, plus their yields are higher because their climate's more forgiving. I think that we just have to be settled into the notion that we're going to have high farming costs and low yields, therefore you shoot for the highest quality you can do.
■ ADAM CAMPBELL

In the vineyard, nature plays a big role, and there is not much you can do about it. You have to learn to deal with what Mother Nature gives. You cannot control how much rain you are going to get, how much heat you are going to get, how many days it's going to freeze or when it's going to freeze. You can try to mitigate those things, but our ability to modify those things is so miniscule compared to what nature can do.

But there is one factor that never changes: people. If you have good people; you are going to do better. The quality of the people, the knowledge of the people is so fundamental. First of all in the vineyard, in our case, we touch the vines, somewhere around twenty-five times a year: pruning, conditioning the shoot, thinning, spraying, cultivating, and on and on. If people make the wrong decision, it's going to affect the crop, not just this year, but next year and maybe the year after. It's people. The wine doesn't make itself. ■ BERNARD LACROUTE

The vineyard teaches you to be observant to what is going on. The vineyard will tell you a lot if you spend some time there. But you can't just drive by; you have to get out in it. Then the vineyard will tell you about plant health, what the crop looks like. You observe how hot it is. Does it need irrigation, what do the clusters look like? ■ CHRIS BANEK

My brother Ted, our vineyard manager, says as a grower, he's growing grape skins. Most of the flavor and aroma is in the skin. ■ TERRY CASTEEL

One year at harvest two guys were getting grapes from one field, one in the morning and one in the afternoon. I was thinking about when to pick this field. The one guy in the morning said, "There's no flavor, there's just no flavor, Allen." I said, "Okay, yep, there's no flavor." The guy that came out in the afternoon goes, "This is wonderful, let's pick it." Like . . . okay.

Naturally, I do what they say. But I have a trick. The winemaker will look to see what other winemakers are doing. Voices start working: "Are they picking?" and "What's going on over there?" ■ ALLEN HOLSTEIN

To make really good wine, you need to harvest at the right time. To do that, you've got to be out there, not only be doing your chemistry to determine the sugar acid balance, phenolics, and all that stuff; but you've got to listen to the fruit when it's telling you, "I'm ready." You hear the "I'm ready" when the fruit gets soft, the little basal leaves turn yellow, the stem of the cluster has turned brown or is beginning to turn, the seeds inside are brown instead of green and when you pull the berries off of the stem, they don't take any of the pulp out with them. Then they're ready. ■ TERRY CASTEEL

〜 OPPOSITE: Close-up of Pinot noir tendril wrapped around larger stem in Adelsheim's Bryan Creek Vineyard near Newberg, Oregon.
ABOVE: Close-up of spider and reflection of photographer on Pinot noir grapes at Amity Vineyards near Amity in Yamhill County, Willamette Valley.

Human beings have been involved in agricultural activity, let's say, for tens of thousands of years. When did we stop being organic? A hundred years ago, a hundred and ten? The rest of human history, it's always been organic. Yet we call this recent petrochemical-based farming conventional, and people approach me somewhat incredulously asking, "How can you farm organically? Don't you need the chemicals?"

When we put toxins into the environment, we send out unaccounted costs into the environment. We'll say, "Well, it's cheaper. We can make the wine cheaper this way." But downstream it kills fish, it kills amphibians, it kills birds. Did we make a good deal for anybody? No, we didn't, we made a bad deal and we passed the costs around, looked innocent, and have done damage to the future with that kind of behavior.

Our responsibility on this earth starts here in our own backyard. Obviously, what we do flows downstream, and it goes through the air and eventually it may even end up in a wine bottle in Florida. ■ ED KING III

ᔕ ABOVE: Wire tightener cinches the wires holding Pinot noir vines at Van Duzer Vineyards Winery near Dallas, Willamette Valley. OPPOSITE: Picker cuts Merlot grapes at Abacela Vineyards in the Umpqua region of southern Oregon.

Since we are doing everything organically, we grow without using any synthetic pesticides or fertilizers. For weed control, everything is done mechanically. It used to be hand hoeing. I did a lot of hand hoeing when I first came here. We did about two rows a day; it was hard work. The grass was really established and had a good root system, so when you hit it with the hoe, you would pull out big clods. Over the years we developed different techniques using a tractor, and now it takes a couple hours an acre. ■ MELITON MARTINEZ

As a human you can look at a vineyard that is manicured, it's all mowed down. There's not a single weed under the vine. It may look good and satisfy you as a human, but it's not looking good towards balancing the ecosystem of the insect life that needs to be there. So you go to my vineyard it may look a little bit messy with tall grass in places but I can assure you that it is tended with intent. ■ SCOTT SHULL

The idea of composting is to replace what you're taking away from the soil at harvest. If you own the vineyard, grow the fruit, and sell it to a winery, you're exporting things off of that property. If you don't put something back in, it tends to catch up with you after time. You're mining things out of the soil, and it needs to be replaced. Composting is an easy way to do that because you're taking what came off and you're putting it right back on again. ■ JOHN ALBIN

The thing I like about biodynamics is the concept of taking from nature and putting back into nature. We do the very same things that organic farmers do, cover cropping, companion plants, integration of animals into the farm, composting, cultivating, and things of that nature. So that's the biological part of biodynamic farming.

On top of that is the dynamic part, which considers the movement of planets and the stars. Many plants grow faster at night under moonlight—which of course is reflected light from the sun—than during the day.

The premise to biodynamics is that plants get their energy from the whole universe. In biodynamic farming you don't just look at the microcosm, you look at the macrocosm. The whole universe affects our lives and the planet where we are living. As a living organism, a biodynamic farm should also be self-sustaining. Therefore, the goal of any biodynamic farm is to reduce the amount of outsourced inputs, and eventually eliminate the need altogether. This is especially important with wine, as the maintenance of a unique sense of place is essential to maintain the vineyard's sense of terroir. A healthy farm would be one that could produce everything it needs from within itself. ■ MOE MOMTAZI

having a family with eight kids. You have the good ones and bad ones; they're all yours you know. Likewise some clones are just better behaved than others. Some like to stay out at night and…So hopefully you know what those traits are before you put them in the ground. ■ DICK ERATH

I had no idea when I developed the Scott Henry trellis system that it was unique. I thought that after two thousand years of growing grapes someone's come up with it, I just didn't know about it. My trellis system allows grape production on rich valley soils; it pretty much shot to hell the old theory

that rich ground wasn't great for wine. Since we were growing grapes in the valley floor, for us it was just a matter of addressing the problem that rich ground produced a lot of plant growth, something you don't want when producing premium grapes. After looking at all the possibilities, we said: "Let's spread the fruit out. We'll go to two levels of fruit on each vine." That way the fruit's not crowded and we can double the crop load.
■ CALVIN SCOTT HENRY III

We've just scratched the surface of great vineyard sites. People are experimenting with higher elevations and steeper grades, and we're certainly looking to double our vineyard acreage in the next five years, all on what might be the best vineyard site in Oregon. We don't know. I think that's exciting. In Burgundy all the sites are taken. There you can make your little area as good as you can make it, but there's certainly no chance of finding a new site. We have planted so little of our potential great vineyard sites in Oregon. The best vineyard site in Oregon probably hasn't been planted yet. ■ ADAM CAMPBELL

There are these moments of vineyard zen where you just feel at one with the universe. I can remember the first time it happened to me. We were harvesting. It was dark, hours after the sun had gone down. We were almost done. I got on the tractor to go dump some stems from the destemmer/crusher and I'm driving through the vineyard with the tractor lights on. I can only see what's directly ahead of me. So I wondered if I can see with the lights turned off. I turn the lights off and it was this completely magical moment where the moon illuminated the entire field. I could see everything, the entire vineyard, by moonlight. I got back up to the rest of the guys and told them it was like talking with God. They said, "Well, we gotcha. There's no turning back now." They were right. ■ EVAN BELLINGAR

ꝏ OPPOSITE: Worker on tractor spreads grass seed for a cover crop between rows of Pinot blanc and Pinot gris at Adelsheim's Bryan Creek Vineyard near Newberg. ABOVE: Scott Henry III, shows the double trellis system he developed to cope with the rich valley soils of his Henry Estate Winery Vineyards. Now his trellis is used throughout the world. Henry Estate Winery Vineyards are next to Umpqua River, in the Umpqua AVA.

ABOVE: Birdhouse in Maresh vineyard near Dundee, Willamette Valley. Martha Maresh built dozens of houses for endangered bluebirds, but a wide variety of birds have moved in. RIGHT: Harvest foreman dumps a bucket of Merlot grapes during harvest at Abacela Vineyards & Winery near Roseburg.

Chapter 5

The Wine and the Winemaker

I n Oregon, if you're making the best quality Pinot noir, that just might be the best Pinot noir made in the world that year. I think that any given year, the best Pinot could be from Oregon or it could be from Burgundy, maybe from New Zealand, maybe from California. ■ ADAM CAMPBELL

Every year is a different year. That's Oregon. If every year were the same here it would be pretty boring, and I would be doing something else. It's like photography. Ansel Adams said the film negative was the score to the music and the print was the performance. It's the same thing with grapes. Every year Mother Nature gives you this negative. Okay, we've got these grapes; here's what you've got to work with. Then you take them into the winery and create the performance. ■ DICK ERATH

Don't trust a winemaker who doesn't have dirty feet at harvest time.
■ BOB MCRITCHIE

ဢ OPPOSITE: Winemaker and owner Tim Schechtel in the brick basement of the Erin Glenn Winery in the historic The Mint building in downtown The Dalles. Although the building was originally commissioned by President Abraham Lincoln in 1864 as a US mint, it never functioned as one.

I am the wine grower rather than the wine maker. I think it's a bit arrogant to say I make the wine. It connotes a philosophy of the person who is in control of everything. My philosophy is a bit different. I certainly have ownership and accountability. But Mother Nature has a big part in this as well. It's the vine and what takes place in the vineyard. I'm just the janitor and shepherd of the process. ■ SCOTT SHULL

Most of my energy as winemaker is spent out here in the vineyard. That's where the wine gets made. Being a winemaker is sort of like being a midwife. Don't drop the baby. Sometimes when there are complications the doctor has to step in—the winemaker has to step in to fix problems. Otherwise, just let the wine become. Man didn't invent winemaking. This is a God given gift. Wine happens all on its own. My job is: don't mess it up. ■ STEVEN WESTBY

∽ ABOVE: Worker stirring the lees or sediments that gather at the bottom during fermentation in 6,000-gallon stainless steel tanks at King Estate Winery south of Eugene. OPPOSITE: A glass wine thief used to draw wine from the barrel and glass of red wine sit on top of a barrel in the underground Adelsheim Winery cellar near Newberg.

In winemaking there is a confluence between supreme idealism and the ugly reality of life that sometimes you have to face. There is a very practical nature of making wine, which is very kind of craftsman. It's not always the artist winemaker or the science winemaker. Sometimes it's just the guy who's got to make this busted thing work and has to figure out a solution to a problem that doesn't seem to want to be solved. ■ MARK VLOSSAK

For me it's all about flavor development. You can buy sugar, you can add water, you can add tartaric acid, but you can't buy a bag of flavor. When I pick, I don't even test in the winery anymore. I just taste the grapes, and that's my guide. Now, that is not to say that when it's pouring, and I'm standing at the French doors of the winery at three in the morning thinking about the hundred tons that I still have hanging out there in the vineyard, that I don't have some anxiety about my decision making. I do. ■ PATTY GREEN

I honestly thought that I would have gone back to California by now. I came up here for the experience but, honestly, I was in no way committed to the longevity of it. Now I will never go back, and part of it is the fruit that we are able to produce up here. At wineries where I've worked in the past, there was not as much balance in the fruit as in what we get off of the vine here. Here, I really enjoy making wine, not manipulating it. I feel more of a connection with the fruit because you're really letting the fruit speak for itself in the wine. ■ LINDSAY KAMPFF

⌘ LEFT: Winemaker Lynn Penner-Ash writing notes during a tasting at Penner-Ash Wine Cellars in the Willamette Valley. ABOVE TOP: Winemaker Dave Paige checking one of his wines in the barrel room at Adelsheim Winery, Willamette Valley.
ABOVE: Winemakers Mike Eyres and Harry Peterson-Nedry checking the color of a Pinot noir with a flashlight at Chehalem Winery near Newberg in the Willamette Valley.

The wines have gotten better over the years and I think it's a matter of the vineyards getting older and in many ways the winemaker is getting older and wiser as well. ■ DICK O'BRIEN

Even though I don't like to emphasize it, one of the things that drove me to making wine is that wine approaches immortality. I don't think we are immortal, but I think some of the things we do in life can qualify for at least some degree of immortality. The immortality isn't the wine itself, it's that you've left something behind; it's like leaving a piece of literature or a musical work or an art piece. I like to think that what is in the bottle is a piece of art. ■ HARRY PETERSON-NEDRY

A perfect bottle of wine gives you shivers. I get shivers still. When you taste the wine, you can just feel it. It's kind of an internal gut feeling. But I'm always wondering if I could have done a better job. I'm constantly second-guessing myself and wanting to try again. Can we reblend that? You can ask these guys that work here; I drive them nuts because we'll taste the same blend in various forms ten times before I'll finally say, "Okay I think maybe we need to go ahead and pursue blend B." I'm always wondering if there isn't yet a better bottle of wine out there. ■ LYNN PENNER-ASH

Assuming that we have selected the clones properly, and we're producing really good grapes, the winemaker's role is not to detract from that quality. I remember a comment that Dick Erath made some years ago. When Domaine Drouhin opened, they had an industry-only opening. When I got there, I was going downstairs, and Erath was coming up. I said, "Hey Dick, just right off the top of your head, I don't want you to even think about it, just give me an answer. How are the wines?" He said, "Bill, they are really good Oregon Pinot noirs. If they would have been Burgundy, I would have been pissed." ■ BILL FULLER

In the inclement years especially, deciding when to pick is paramount. So my hamster wheel goes constantly and my stomach grinds. It's totally anxiety ridden. The way I deal with it is to actually get out in the vineyard and taste the grapes over and over and over. In the end, you have to trust intuition to make that final decision. ■ ROLLIN SOLES

There are two fermentations that the wine goes through: the primary fermentation, the big active fermentation where the fruit juice gets turned into wine, and the malolactic fermentation, a second, more gentle and long fermentation that happens in the barrel room.

∽ OPPOSITE: Winegrower Jason Lett in The Eyrie Vineyards Winery chemistry lab in McMinnville.
ABOVE: A thermometer measures the temperature of grape juice in a stainless steel tank in the Carlton Winemakers Studio production area in Carlton, Willamette Valley. The facility is set up for use by a variety of winemakers and wineries.

In 1974, Dad had his first spontaneous malolactic fermentation. The bacteria was just something flying around in the air that liked the way the winery smelled, so it came in and lived here. In fact, if you look up at the ceiling there, the splat mark right over that barrel, that's the wine splatter I made when I was about sixteen. I was washing a barrel and I had stuck one of the bungs too tight in the barrel with fermenting Chardonnay. The gas pressure built up, and it went kaboosh! A huge fountain of wine shot straight up at the ceiling. Then the bacteria said, "Oh great, free treats." So they moved in and colonized that splat area.

It turns out this cellar has some special characteristics; so now you can commercially buy strains of the bacteria from our ceiling. There is a French-based fermentation supply company that sells it all over the world. Actually, about one-half of it is the Eyrie strain they refined here, and the other half is from Erath. So the two of us live in the same envelope together that is shipped all around the world. ■ JASON LETT

■ ABOVE: Steam cleaning oak barrels before they are filled with wine at Penner-Ash Winery in the Willamette Valley near Newberg. OPPOSITE: Winemaker Véronique Drouhin-Boss using a hydrometer to check the sugar levels in the wine at Domaine Drouhin Oregon, Willamette Valley.

I had only a brief two years in the limelight when I made Robert Parker's favorite wine. He fell in love with my 1983 winemaker's reserve; so I went through a period where I was the object of cork and dork worship. But I refused to release my 1983 winemaker's reserve when Parker declared it: "The best Pinot I had seen inside of Oregon." I didn't think it was ready, and I wasn't going to release my wines according to the dictates of some famous wine writer. Of course, you don't stay in the focus very long because the wine critic moves along to write about the next person. So I sat on it until the glow was gone and then released it. It still sold okay. ■ MYRON REDFORD

I spend a lot of time with a big piece of paper saying, "Okay if we transfer Tank One to Tank Ten, then Two can handle the fruit from this vineyard. But now wait a minute, do we have enough barrels ready?" It's a chess game because

you ultimately know down the road you're going to back yourself in a corner somewhere, and you try not to let that happen. You don't want to be checkmate. ■ LYNN PENNER-ASH

A lot of people call me to ask what it takes to be a winemaker. One of the first things I ask is: Are you married? Do you have a family? How's the relationship because this is going to stress it out. People are always incredibly shocked when I ask them. But it's true. Notice, I'm not married. ■ PATTY GREEN

In 2001, when I was working for Willamette Valley Vineyards, I worked for seventy-one days straight. It's tough on the spouse when you have kids. And you get home sticky and wet. It's really a labor of love, of passion. ■ JOE DOBBES

⚬ BELOW: Winemaker John Guerrero adjusts the bilge hoop on a French oak barrel at Valley View Winery in the Applegate Valley. OPPOSITE: Owner and winemaker Bernard Lerch "punching down" the cap of skins and pulp back into the juice during fermentation at Hood River Winery in the Columbia River Gorge. The winemaker wants skin-to-juice contact to give red and fruit wines their color and tannins. This is said to be the oldest winery in the Gorge.

When we started production in our southern Oregon facility in 1989, I was the winemaker. In 1991 I fired myself and hired a good winemaker. I fired myself because many times I would say, "Oh that's good enough." In the winery that's not a good attitude to have. You need someone who is going for 100 percent. ■ TED GERBER

In 1990, when I had just started at Hinman Vineyards, I was doing a diatomaceous earth filtration. After I had run a successful filtration, I valved it off to clean it. This filter was new to me and there were all these nozzles, hoses and valves. Well, I forgot to close the water valve. When I turned on the pump, it was strong enough to push wine up into the winery's plumbing system and into these two large water-holding tanks. The Hinman family lived right next door and was also drawing water out of those two tanks. So about 8:30 at night, Ann Hinman called me, "Joe there's wine coming out of the water system. There's wine pouring into the kid's bathtub."

Sure enough. I ran over to the filter, so I closed down the valve.

That was mighty good tasting water. I lost about 300 gallons. ■ JOE DOBBES

I've made Chardonnay every year that we have been a winery. But I went through some bumps in the road trying to make Burgundian-style Chardonnay. In 2003, I dumped it all down the drain because it was too alcoholic and big. It tasted like I failed at trying to make a California Chardonnay. It tasted like a lemon meringue pie. I was so frustrated I stopped making Chardonnay for two years.

I was fortunate to meet David and Jason Lett, and they sold me fruit from the Eyrie vineyard. I learned a lot about Chardonnay from one of Oregon's masters, but I had to go through that total failure to achieve success. ■ JOSH BERGSTRÖM

Many people pooh-pooh Oregon Chardonnay. What they have forgotten is the very first Oregon wine to make *Wine Spectator*'s Top 100 giants of the year was my 1989 Chardonnay. ■ BILL FULLER

Probably my biggest disappointment is that, since the mid-1980s, wines have become these monsters. They are oaky, they are dark color, they are high in alcohol, more everything. They don't taste like Pinot noir. Pinot noir is diaphanous, a woman you want to dance with, instead of sumo wrestle with. ■ DAVID LETT

One economic point important to Oregon is that we cannot compete with Pinot noir from California. They get six tons of grapes to the acre. Our high end here is about three tons to the acre. So the economics just put us in a different price category. We just can't compete with the California $7.99, $8.99, or $9.99 bottle. The economics are not in our favor starting from the vineyard. ■ LAURENT MONTALIEU

When the winegrower goes to plant a vineyard, he designs in his head what he wants the wine to taste like. If he's designing a twenty-dollar wine, he's going to plant for larger yields. If he's planting for a hundred-dollar wine, he wants very dense yields. That's the difference between a farmer and a winegrower. The grower grows the wine he wants to make. ■ GARY ANDRUS

꙳ OPPOSITE: Winemaker Terry Casteel in the barrel room at Bethel Heights Vineyard winery, Eola Hills, Willamette Valley. LEFT: Partially filled wine glasses with marked bottles in background are all part of a winemaker's blending test at Willamette Valley Vineyards near Turner, Willamette Valley.

Chapter 6

The Future

One time we were barrel tasting up at Domaine Drouhin, when they made their first wine. I wrote a little note to Robert, the owner: "Robert, I tasted your wines. They're phenomenal. We've been in the business for twenty years. You've been in it for probably two hundred years. I appreciate the fact that you people have been doing it for two hundred years, we're not there yet. We don't claim to be there yet. We're only 180 years behind. But some day we'll catch up." ■ JIM MARESH

Oregon arguably was the first region in America developed as a wine region because it looked like the right place scientifically to be growing grapes. Washington could essentially make the same claim, but Oregon really fit the niche. That's why the modern-era pioneers came here; Richard Sommer and David Lett were motivated to move to a cooler growing region. At that time they were clearly the lunatic fringe and it took a long time for us to get beyond that label. But we started to make some pretty good wines, not because we were particularly good winemakers, but because we had really good raw materials to work with. ■ KEVIN CHAMBERS

It's really hard to know where the Oregon wine industry will be in one hundred years, but I think that the Willamette Valley grows a variety in a style which appeals to a very narrow part of the palate. Where southern Oregon

OPPOSITE: Old cash register at Hillcrest Winery, originally established by Richard Sommer in 1961, as Bonded Winery No 44, it is considered to be the oldest estate winery since Prohibition, Umpqua AVA.

ℐ Opposite: Close-up of Pinot noir grapes with morning dew drops in the Nicholas Vineyard on the Chehalem Ridge of the Willamette Valley near Newberg. Above: An aerial view of vineyards in the hills near Dundee, Willamette Valley.

☙ OPPOSITE: Sunrise light hits a variety of vineyards in the Red Hills above Dundee, Willamette Valley. LEFT: Cabernet Sauvignon grapes ready for harvest at Valley View Winery vineyard in southern Oregon's Applegate Valley.

and eastern Oregon have climates and growing conditions that serve a much bigger part of the palate: the Cabernets, Syrahs, and Merlots. So in a hundred years, the Willamette Valley might become a little Burgundy, and the rest of Oregon might be where the action is, where the economic and industry growth takes place. It's very possible that the center of gravity will change. ■ JIM BERNAU

The north end of the Willamette Valley, I think, is where we're really going to see a big facelift because of the wine industry. It's the most densely concentrated area. You can already see Dundee is changing, Newberg is changing, McMinnville is beginning to change. There's more money coming in. Those towns will be centered around servicing the wine industry. ■ BEN CASTEEL

I think the major unknown viticulturally is going to be the east side of the state, and what potentially could happen around Walla Walla, Hermiston, Pendleton, Boardman, and Milton-Freewater. There's probably around ten thousand acres out there on the Oregon side that's going for about a hundred dollars an acre. Right now it's wheat land, but it's probably world-class vineyard land that would equal anything in Washington today. Someone will have to throw their arms around it and in ten or twenty years establish an AVA. They'll make it into the history books and change the history of the Oregon wine. ■ ED KING III

∽ ABOVE: A weathered lichen-covered wooden sign identifies the grape varietal at a Valley View Winery vineyard near Ruch, southern Oregon. OPPOSITE: A long photographic exposure created these "star trails" over a vineyard near Sherwood, Willamette Valley.

In the long term, southern Oregon has expanded at a much slower pace than the Willamette Valley but in the immediate term it's a different story. Five years ago we had twenty wineries and today we have close to sixty, and we will probably eclipse one hundred wineries in the next three years. That is all good for the state of Oregon in general and for southern Oregon specifically. ■ MICHAEL DONOVAN

There are a lot of fundamental economic reasons why Oregon's wine industry will remain fairly small, independent, and high quality. Large corporations scratch their heads and worry about the risks of entering this market. We have less predictable conditions, we have fewer opportunities to mechanize, we have fewer opportunities for scale, and we have low yields. All those things frustrate large corporations. ■ JIM BERNAU

In the future, I think Oregon will look like much of the wine industry in the United States, with a certain number of relatively large enterprises, which principally feed the world of distribution. Hopefully, there'll also be some middle-tier wineries that also feed distribution, but at a higher price point and a higher level of expectation. Then there'll be large numbers of small enterprises that sell their wine directly to consumers. It's hard for me to believe that model will change. ■ DAVID ADELSHEIM

One of the problems with growing bigger as an industry is that we can't get everybody in the firehouse any more. The industry size may put a damper on

ꕥ ABOVE: **Close-up of a lady bug, a symbol for sustainable agriculture, on green Pinot noir grapes at Beran Winery vineyard, Willamette Valley.** OPPOSITE: **Barrel room at King Estate Winery located south of Eugene.**

the collaborative Oregon spirit. However, I don't think that is going to happen because of the new AVAs.

They have successfully taken a large concentration of wineries and vineyards—more than three hundred wineries and six hundred vineyards—and divided them into at least six pieces. So now Ribbon Ridge has about twenty vineyards and wineries. Can twenty people get together to do things collaboratively? You bet your butt. The Dundee Hills, the Eola Hills, they are now manageable sizes so that people can actually sit down and put their heads together. Yeah, there's going to be a little bit of semi-competing between the AVAs, but in general people know that if you stick together, you're going to be a lot more powerful than if you try to do it alone. ■ HARRY PETERSON-NEDRY

Land and property values are challenging us. The price is too high. Just five years ago, a lot of these acres out here sold for a third of today's price. When you put that in your fiscal budget, you start to wonder, "Ah man, I don't know if this makes sense." ■ LYNN PENNER-ASH

The biggest threat to an ongoing Oregon wine industry is that our countryside and farmlands are so beautiful, so desirable, that everybody wants to live there. Everyone wants to build a big house on top of a hill and look down on the vineyards. I think it's scary not to protect vineyard lands the same way we protect bottomlands in the valley. ■ HARRY PETERSON-NEDRY

We see Portland growing rapidly. It's under great pressure to accommodate a huge influx of people who recognize it as a wonderful city. It's maybe the top American city today, at least in the top three or five, in terms of livability and quality of life. While we have a significant number of land use restrictions, if we were to add a half a million or a million people to the current Portland urban growth boundary—I don't know that anything is sufficient to withstand the influx of that many people. Many of those people are going to explore every nook and cranny to find a place to live out of the city.

∾ LEFT: Father Richard with worker David Martinez on the bottling line in the wine warehouse at the Our Lady of the Guadalupe Trappist Abbey near Lafayette, Willamette Valley. This former furniture making facility has been converted as a storage facility for cases of wine from wineries all over the Willamette Valley. RIGHT: Two families enjoy a picnic and wine among the Sokol Blosser Winery vineyards near Dundee, Oregon.

The wine industry is going to have to fight all along the way. Economics won't protect the vineyards. We've seen valuable vineyard land in Napa that is still more valuable for houses. The same is going to be true around Portland, if we let economics run the game. You could see the vineyards of McMinnville, Dundee, Carlton, Eola Hills all overwhelmed by the demand for housing. You could end up with this kind of vineyard in a terrarium, with a little glass dome over the cute little winemaker's old pickup truck and his dog. You drive out and pay your fee to see them. It's like a visit to the zoo. ■ ED KING III

One thing is sure, I don't think we will have Prohibition again. I think we have passed that stage. ■ PHILIPPE GIRARDET

Chapter 7

The Lessons
from the Vineyard

The vineyard has made me an optimist. There is the rebirth, the variation, through the seasons. I've learned that if things don't go well this year, they will go better next year. This is after experiencing the variation of many vintages. ■ DICK PONZI

Getting out into the vineyard was a life-changing event for me. I could have lived my whole life in the city never realizing the connection to the land that I felt when I got out into the vineyard. That's where I first realized how much we are simply part of nature and the connection between all things. We needed to work with nature, not simply crush it. Take a seed; how does that seed know to grow into a bean? It has to have the whole idea of what happens in the seed. What a miracle. So the vineyards are my passion. They've made me a nature person. ■ SUSAN SOKOL BLOSSER

The vineyard has taught me many lessons, but the most powerful is the proper role for myself, and all human beings, in the cycle of life on Earth.

When you're tending a vine, which lives for eighty years, when you're planting a vineyard that will live for hundreds of years, when you're working with

OPPOSITE: Close-up of old-vine Pinot noir in Lett's Eyrie Winery vineyard, planted in 1974, near Dundee, Willamette Valley.

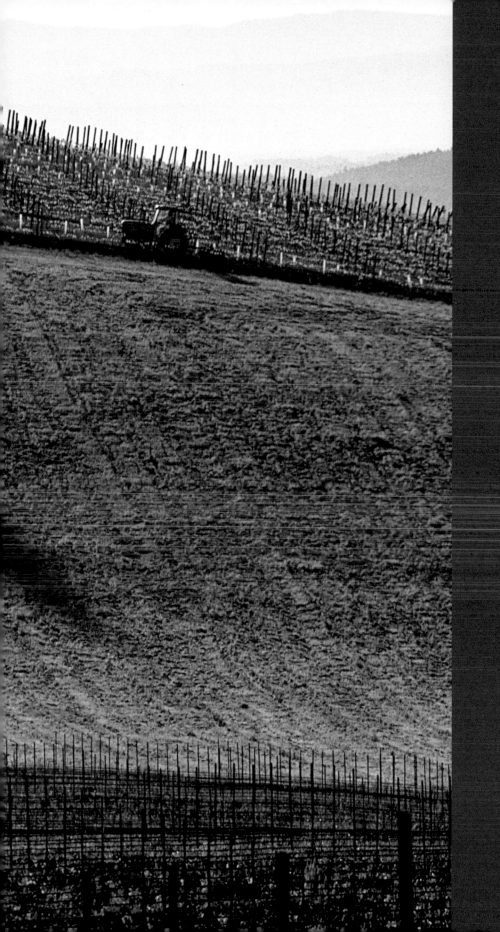

➷ OPPOSITE: Tractor in vineyard with dramatic shadow in Red Hills above Dundee. ABOVE: Harvesting Pinot gris during the rain at Henry Estate Winery vineyards in the Umpqua AVA of southern Oregon.

↩ ABOVE: **A mechanical cutter pruning back the vines at Domaine Drouhin, Willamette Valley.**

the soil and the environment that needs to be preserved for thousands of years, you might not see the result of your own actions and sacrifices in your lifetime.

With that perspective, my role, no, duty, is to be responsible to that land and all the living creatures into the future, well beyond my own lifespan. When we properly discharge our stewardship, everyone is rewarded in the short and long term. It could be preventing soil erosion, or preserving the microflora—the life in the soil—or protecting the groundwater from chemicals or silt, or immediate little things like setting up machinery to protect workers' hands from danger or even not irritating the neighbors.

With this vineyard perspective, I realize that the decisions I make are part of a bigger play. ■ JIM BERNAU

The vineyard has taught me about people. As the vineyard manager I get it from all ends; from the people who are doing the field work, from the wine-maker, from the wine customers who can afford the $100 bottle of wine, from the vineyard owners who have their own vision, and from the press who come from New York. It's fun to talk with those people from those different environments. ■ CHRIS BANEK

I would say, for our whole family, that we really learned a lesson about sustainability from the vineyard. It's an issue much bigger than our Bethel Heights operation, or even the Oregon wine industry. To me it's almost a cultural crisis.

We can't look at this place as being a dumping ground for chemicals and other inputs that, in a short term, might produce more grapes or more wine. We have to look at this place as self-sustaining over a long period of time; we're talking generations.

Here's an example. We had cutworms here our first year. A cutworm is a little insect that eats the growing tip of the grape vine. The farm service guy told us to spray with this product called Sevin. My wife said, "I don't like it. The only thing I ask is that we not spray the whole vineyard, leave a section unsprayed so we can use it for comparison." So the next year the only place we didn't have a cutworm problem was the place we didn't spray. With the spray, we killed all the bugs, even the good ones. That's one of the lessons that I've been taught in the vineyard. ■ TERRY CASTEEL

Vineyards have taught me patience: you live with the seasons, not faster, not slower. There I have learned that you enjoy the life you live when you live the life you like. I love making wine even though the romance is not always there! ■ VÉRONIQUE DROUHIN-BOSS

Every year the vineyard teaches me about renewal; about having a second chance, or a third chance, or a fourth chance, or a twenty-seventh chance to do it right. You aren't always burdened by what the last harvest has been, by what the last death of a child has been. There is always hope because there's a new season. ■ HARRY PETERSON-NEDRY

I think the vineyard humbles people. You think you have control over your destiny or the quality of your fruit, but there will always be challenges. It's how you rise to those challenges that really defines character and, in the long run, defines quality of the product. ■ RON PENNER-ASH

The vineyard doesn't talk to me, it doesn't teach me, per se, but it forces me to learn, and I tend to learn from people. I didn't get a handle on this one vineyard site until I went to Germany and stood next to a twelve-year-old boy whose family made wine. He tasted my Pinot gris and said, "Oh, one typical aging." I had no idea what he was talking about, but that started an investigation that led us to understand what drought stress does, particularly to white wines. It helped us understand how to farm that site, ultimately to make dense red wine, and incredibly rich white wines. ■ DAVID ADELSHEIM

This is getting pretty metaphysical for a scientist, but Pinot noir is almost a religion, a spiritual thing, an enlightening thing for me. I'm not an artist. I can't play horn or piano, I can't carry a tune in a bucket, I can't even paint by numbers, but I have artistic sense about the spirituality in the wine. Nature and organic farming allows me to bring all the land gives if I live with it and

ᴓ ABOVE: First vineyard manager at Domaine Drouhin, Allen Holstein, collects grapes to take to the lab at Domaine Drouhin, Willamette Valley. The white reflective tarp under his feet reflects heat onto the grapes to effectively extend the ripening day.

 ABOVE: A round plastic sign tacked at the end of a row identifies the vines to be 777 clone of Pinot noir in Elton Vineyard owned by Dick and Betty O'Brian, in Yamhill County, Willamette Valley. OPPOSITE: Early morning fog over fall-colored Knudsen Vineyard seen from Bella Vida Vineyard in the Red Hills above Dundee, Oregon. Foreground vines are Dijon clone Pinot noir.

taste it all the time. That gives me a presence of creation. Then I get to share that enlightening experience in the wine with others. ■ GARY ANDRUS

Vineyards are like children. They have good years. They have bad years. Through it all they need loving attention. We have to keep training them every year. We have to see what they are doing all of the time. We need to hover over them constantly. And they never grow up. ■ GRACE EVENSTAD

The vineyard has taught me that you need to love what you do. For example, these Oregon wine growers have given up other careers and life choices to do what they do. They love it. That's why I think we see in these people this joy for their life choice. That certainly is a wonderful thing for all of us to learn. ■ SUE HORSTMANN

We have people here who started out with two million dollars, but now have one million dollars because they planted a vineyard. ■ MIGUEL LOPEZ

The vineyard has taken me on a path that has brought me closer and closer to nature. I find that many things I do in my spare time now involve trees, plants, and birds. A lot of it is about conservation. I never envisioned myself being that attached to nature, but the vineyard has definitely taken me in that direction. I think all those things are very satisfying and very enriching for my life. ■ PAT CAMPBELL

The vineyard always provides new challenges. For example, this year it's the weather. We had such a crazy spring. It snowed in April, then a week later it was 100 degrees. Everyday is different. ■ TRAUTE MOORE

It takes a little while to get the rhythm of some plants. Like the Riesling over there. I cut on that hard the first year and it made stunning wine, but the Cabernet just didn't. It was one of those moments that made me realize this is one of the great lessons that the vineyard and the wine teach: It's all in due time. It's not like get in there, go bang, bang, bang, bang, and that's it.

It's like kids. If you spend time with them, teach them things, then when they're eighteen, they have a work ethic and are curious about life. They'll do well for themselves. If you set them on the couch, give them Cap'n Crunch, and kick them out at eighteen, they'll fall on their face. Vines are the same way. They need to be brought up in the way you want them to act as adults; so I want to have plants that are very slow and methodical. ■ DYSON DEMARA

The vineyard has taught me to look at the world differently, really differently, than when I was a television reporter. Since living right in the middle of the vineyard and working with the vines and the wines, I've become a lot more tuned to the seasons, to the natural cycles, to nature, to the moon, to the rain-fall, to all those things. I love all of that. It takes me back to my childhood when I grew up as a nature boy in the woods by the Willamette River. Then I became an adult, a creature of the world, of the modern city. I left all of the childhood nature behind.

Living in this vineyard and making wine brings me back to the childhood time, to a lot of things I was sensitive to as a kid. I like that. I am very content now. ■ DOUG TUNNELL

I am a perfectionist. If you are a perfectionist, the grape can drive you crazy. Grapes want to be wild, you know. Perfection is a nice goal but you have to get perspective. There is a point that you have to let go, let life take its course. I resigned my post as director of the universe. ■ PHILIPPE GIRARDE

ৰ্চ OPPOSITE: A tractor works the Ribbon Ridge Estate vineyard at family owned Aramenta Cellars near Newberg, Willamette Valley. ABOVE: A yellow tractor-crossing sign at the vineyard entrance to Domaine Drouhin Oregon Winery.

I've learned that sunscreen is an essential part of life. ■ LAURA LOTSPEICH

The vineyard teaches me that very little that I think is under my control, is really under my control. It teaches me to live with that uncertainty. Agriculture is all about gambling. ■ MYRON REDFORD

In the vineyard I learned to be prepared for adversity. It might have made me more conservative in my train of thought. The negative side is that it tends to dominate my character. My daughter complains that I'm too conservative when I won't jump on the trampoline with her. But in the vineyard you have to think out what you are going to do. You can't just do a 180 in the middle of a job that's going to take you three days to complete. ■ JIM KAKACEK

Growing up in the vineyard I learned that if you work hard, you reap rewards. If you pruned a particular vineyard and you did all the work there from pruning to harvest, then at the end of harvest you can say, "I pruned that vine right there. I made sure it made it through the winter and that it made it through the spring. I properly positioned all of the shoots. I properly made sure it was alive. "Look at what I've done." That translates to life for me. If I work I will be just fine. Good things will happen, I will benefit. ■ MIGUEL LOPEZ

Artist's Vision

Eddi Miglavs

Contrary to the title, this book is not really about wine. Rather it's about an extraordinary group of individuals who, for some reason, happened to come together in this place called Oregon to create something world-class. It's about their individual and collective energy, their values, their passion, their vision, and their humanness.

From the beginning, I wanted their personal stories to be the narrative, told in their own words. So I set out with recorder and camera. Originally I thought talking with twenty key people would do the trick. Wrong.

In the end, I recorded nearly two hundred hours of interviews with more than eighty owners, winemakers, and vineyard managers from all over the state, and spoke with many more wine-industry workers—in several languages. Then, true to a *National Geographic* background, I took more than three thousand photographs, which I agonizingly edited down to one thousand "finals."

During the very first interview, when I heard Oregon wine pioneer Dick Ponzi say, "I've never really told this to anyone before," I knew we were on the right track. Yes, the factual history of Oregon wine is important, but getting a glimpse of the personalities provides insight into that history. Knowing that David Lett's 1975 South Block Pinot noir trounced the French in two blind tastings is a nice fact, but hearing him interact with his son Jason, who has taken his father's place as the Eyrie winegrower, reveals character. And hearing the humble words of one person who came to this country as an illegal immigrant and went on to become the vineyard manager of one of Oregon's largest vineyards and an American citizen, reveals something big about Oregon and America.

Transcribing all those interviews, then choosing and carefully editing the copy and photographs became a Herculean task. Through their unique voice, I wanted to let each person reveal something more of themselves than just the narrative. Don't be surprised to find words that are not found in *Webster's*. Unfortunately, my slave-master editor kept insisting we only had 128 pages.

Driving back from doing interviews at Willamette Valley Vineyards late one night, I was just reflecting on all that I had heard during the seven months of recording. Somewhere on I-5 North, I suddenly found myself truly inspired by all the stories. This is indeed an amazing group of individuals who mysteriously had come together in Oregon from all parts of the world to create a taste of wine unlike any else on this earth. ■ JĀNIS MIGLAVS

Acknowledgments

Since I was only the humble harvester for this work, I need to thank all of those who made this project possible. First, thank you to my wife Eddi for putting up with my weeks of wandering around Oregon and rolling out at 3:30 in the morning to get the first-light photograph, or leave for Milton-Freewater for an 8:00 A.M. interview. Thank you to all of the patient winemakers, owners, vineyard managers, cellar rats, and field workers who put up with all my questions and the constant request for just one more photo. I also sincerely want to thank Jim Bernau for his perspective, financial and spiritual support of the project. Without him, I would have only done twenty interviews. And thanks to Tim Frew and the others at Graphic Arts, as well as Aaron Lisle and Shelby Zadow for helping me wade through more than 1000 "final" photographs and hundreds of pages of interviews and to Vic Parker for picking up the ball. Also, I can't forget to thank the force, spirit or luck that was constantly with me to make sunlight momentarily break through the leaden blanket of Oregon rain clouds to touch the vineyard just as I clicked the shutter. But most of all, I need to thank the One who created all of the light and owns my every breath and moment.

ABOVE: Sunrise in the vineyards at Melrose Winery in the Umpqua region. NEXT PAGE RIGHT: Judging from the sign showing the distance to various French and Spanish wine-growing regions, Abacela Vineyards & Winery near Roseburg is at the center of it all.

Contributors

David Adelsheim
Owner
Adelsheim Vineyards
Newberg/Willamette Valley

John Albin
Director of Viticulture &
   Winemaking
King Estate
Lorane/Willamette Valley

Gary Andrus
Owner/Winemaker
Gypsy Dancer Estates
Cornelius/Willamette Valley

Jimmy Arterberry Maresh
Owner/Winemaker
Arterberry Maresh Wines
Dundee/Willamette Valley

Chris Banek
Vineyard Manager
Seven Hills Vineyard
Walla Walla Valley/Milton-
   Freewater

Evan Bellingar
Vineyard Manager
Advanced Vineyard Systems
McMinnville/Willamette Valley

Bill and Sharon Beran
Owners
Beran Vineyard
Hillsboro/Willamette Valley

Josh Bergström
Co-owner/Vineyard
   Manager/General
   Manager/Winemaker
Bergström Wines
Newberg/Willamette Valley

Jim Bernau
Founder/Winegrower
Willamette Valley Vineyards
Turner/Willamette Valley

Bill Blosser
Director and Secretary of Board
   of Directors
Sokol Blosser Winery
Dundee/Willamette Valley

Terry and Sue Brandborg
Proprietors
Brandborg Vineyard and Winery
Elkton/Umpqua Valley

Scott Burns, Ph.D.
Professor of Geomorphology,
   Soils, & Environmental Geology
Portland State University

Adam Campbell
Owner/Winemaker
Elk Cove Vineyards
Gaston/Willamette Valley

Pat Campbell
Owner
Elk Cove Vineyards
Gaston/Willamette Valley

Stephen Cary
Winemaker
Yamhill Valley Vineyards
McMinnville/Willamette Valley

Terry Casteel
Cofounder/Winemaker
Bethel Heights
Eola Hills/Willamette Valley

Ben Casteel
Assistant Winemaker
Bethel Heights
Eola Hills/Willamette Valley

Kevin Chambers
Co-CEO Oregon Viticulture Supply
Owner
Resonance Vineyard
Yamhill-Carlton/Willamette Valley

(continued on next page)

- Gardner Chappell
Director
Douglas County Museum
Roseburg

- Dyson DeMara
Owner/Winemaker
Historic Hillcrest Winery
Roseburg/Umpqua Valley

- Joe Dobbes
Founder/Owner/Winemaker
Dobbes Family Estate/Wine by Joe
Dundee/Willamette Valley

- Christina Doerner
Owner
Doerner Vineyards
Roseburg/Umpqua Valley

- Michael Donovan
Managing Director
RoxyAnn Winery
Medford/Rogue Valley

- Véronique Drouhin-Boss
Winemaker
Domain Drouhin Oregon
Dayton/Willamette Valley

- Dick Erath
Winegrower
Founder of Erath Vineyards
    Winery/Prince Hill Vineyards
Dundee/Willamette Valley

- Grace Evenstad
Owner
Domaine Serene
Dundee/Willamette Valley

- Mike Eyres
Co-Winemaker
Chehalem Winery
Newberg/Willamette Valley

- Bill Fuller
Founder/Winemaker
Tualatin Estate Vineyards & Winery
Forest Grove/Willamette Valley

- Ted Gerber
Owner/Manager
Foris Vineyards Winery
Illinois Valley/Rogue Valley

- Philippe Girardet
Founder
Girardet Wine Cellars
Roseburg/Umpqua Valley

- Patty Green
Owner/Winemaker
Patricia Green Cellar
Newberg/Willamette Valley

- Calvin Scott Henry III
Founder
Henry Estate Winery
Umpqua/Umpqua Valley

- Allen Holstein
Wine Grower
Argyle Winery
Dundee/Willamette Valley

- Sue Horstmann
Executive Director Willamette Valley
    Wineries Association
Executive Director Oregon Pinot Camp
Portland

- Earl Jones
Owner
Abacela
Roseburg/Umpqua Valley

- Greg Jones
Associate Professor
Geography Department Southern
    Oregon University
Ashland

- Jim Kakacek
Winemaker/General Manager
Van Duzer Vineyards
Dallas/Willamette Valley

- Lindsay Kampff
Winemaker, Red Wines
King Estate
Lorane/Willamette Valley

- Ed King III
Cofounder/CEO
King Estate
Lorane/Oregon

- Cal Knudsen
Owner
Knudsen Vineyard
Dundee/Willamette Valley

- Bill Kremer
Winemaker
King Estate
Lorane/Willamette Valley

- Bernard Lacroute
Owner
WillaKenzie Estate Winery
Yamhill/Willamette Valley

- Don Lange
Owner/Winemaker
Lange Winery
Dundee/Willamette Valley

- Wendy Lange
Owner/CEO
Lange Winery
Dundee/Willamette Valley

- Jesse Lange
General Manager/Winemaker
Lange Winery
Dundee/Willamette Valley

- Eric Lemelson
Owner
Lemelson Vineyards
Carlton/Willamette Valley

- Bernard Lerch
Owner/Winemaker
Hood River Winery
Hood River/Columbia River Gorge

- David Lett
Founder
The Eyrie Vineyards
McMinnville/Willamette Valley

- Jason Lett
Owner/Winegrower
The Eyrie Vineyards
McMinnville/Willamette Valley

- Ed and Darlene Looney
Owners
Aramenta Cellars
Newberg/Willamette Valley

- Miguel Lopez
Winemaker
Walnut City WineWorks
McMinnville/Willamette Valley

- Laura Lotspeich
Founder/Owner (with husband Kurt)
Pheasant Hill Vineyard
Talent/Rogue Valley

- Jeff Lumpkin
General Manager
Carlton Winemakers Studio
Carlton/Willamette Valley

- Rudy Marchesi
Proprietor
Montinore Estate
Forest Grove/Willamette Valley

- Jim Maresh
Founder/Owner
Maresh Vineyard
Dundee Hills/Willamette Valley

- Martha Maresh
Manager
Maresh Vineyard & Retreat
Dundee Hills/Willamette Valley

- Erle Martin
President
Archery Summit Winery
Dayton/Willamette Valley

- Meliton Martinez
Vineyard Manager
King Estate
Lorane/Willamette Valley

- Norm McKibben
Co-Owner
Seven Hills Vineyard
Milton-Freewater/Walla Walla Valley

- Bob McRitchie, Ph.D.
Retired Winemaker/Professor
McMinnville/Willamette Valley

Contributors

■ Anna Metzinger
Winemaker
Archery Summit
Dayton/Willamette Valley

■ Moe Momtazi
Owner
Momtazi Vineyards/Maysara Winery
McMinnville/Willamette Valley

■ Tahmiene Momtazi
Winemaker
Maysara Winery
McMinnville/Willamette Valley

■ Laurent Montalieu
Owner/Winemaker
Northwest Wine Company/Soléna
   Cellars
McMinnville/Willamette Valley

■ Don & Traute Moore
Founders/Owners
Quail Run Vineyards
Rogue Valley

■ Robert Pamplin
Owner
Anne Amie Vineyards
Carlton/Willamette Valley

■ Wayne and Deedy Parker
Owners
Melrose Vineyards
Roseburg/Umpqua Valley

■ Lynn Penner-Ash
Owner/Winemaker
Penner-Ash Wine Cellars
Newberg/Willamette Valley

■ Ron Penner-Ash
Owner
Penner-Ash Wine Cellars
Newberg/Willamette Valley

■ Harry Peterson-Nedry
Founder/Co-Winemaker
Chehalem Winery
Newberg/Willamette Valley

■ Dick & Betty O'Brien
Founders/Owners
Elton Vineyard
Eola Hills/Willamette Valley

■ Dave Paige
Winemaker
Adelsheim Vineyard
Newberg/Willamette Valley

■ Nick Peirano
Owner
Nick's Italian Cafe
McMinnville

■ Dick & Nancy Ponzi
Founders/Owners
Ponzi Vineyards
Beaverton/Willamette Valley

■ Luisa Ponzi
Winemaker
Ponzi Vineyards
Beaverton/Willamette Valley

■ Maria Ponzi Fogelstrom
National Sales/Marketing Director
Ponzi Vineyards
Beaverton/Willamette Valley

■ Myron Redford
Owner
Amity Vineyards
Amity/Willamette Valley

■ Father Richard
Business Manager
Our Lady of Guadalupe Trappist Abbey
Lafayette/Willamette Valley

■ Tim Schechtel
Owner/Winemaker
Erin Glenn Winery
The Dalles/Columbia River Gorge

■ Greg Shine
Chief Ranger/Historian
Ft. Vancouver National Historic Site
Vancouver, WA

■ Scott Shull
Owner/Wine Grower/General Manager
Raptor Ridge Winery
Carlton-Yamhill/Willamette Valley

■ Annie Shull
Owner/Director of Sales & Marketing
Raptor Ridge Winery
Carlton-Yamhill/Willamette Valley

■ Susan Sokol Blosser
Founder
Sokol Blosser Winery
Dundee/Willamette Valley

■ Rollin Soles
Winemaker/Owner
Argyle Winery
Dundee/Willamette Valley

■ Richard Sommer
Founder/Oregon Wine Pioneer
Hillcrest Vineyard
Roseburg/Umpqua Valley

■ Bill & Cathy Stoller
Founders/Owners
Stoller Vineyards
Dayton/Willamette Valley

■ Milan Stoyanov
Owner
David Hill Winery
Forest Grove/Willamette Valley

■ Lee Traynham
Owner
Del Rio Vineyards and Winery
Gold Hill/Rogue Valley

■ Doug Tunnel
Winemaker/Proprietor
Brick House Vineyards
Newberg/Willamette Valley

■ Mark Vlossak
Founder/President/Winemaker
St. Innocent Winery
Salem/Willamette Valley

■ John Weisinger
Owner/Winemaker
Weisinger's of Ashland
Ashland/Rogue Valley

■ Steven Westby
Winemaker/Vineyard Manager
Witness Tree Vineyard
Salem/Willamette Valley

■ Steven and Allison Whiteside
Proprietors
Bella Vida Vineyard
Dundee/Willamette Valley

■ Mark & Mike Wisnovsky
Co-Owners
Valley View Winery
Jacksonville/Applegate Valley

■ Lonnie Wright
Grape Farmer
The Pines
The Dalles/Columbia River Gorge

■ Ken Wright
Founder/Winemaker
Ken Wright Cellars
Carlton/Willamette Valley

■ Cecil Zerba
Cofounder
Zerba Cellars
Milton-Freewater/Walla Walla Valley